When I Was Your Age

When I Was Your Age

Life Lessons, Funny Stories &
Questionable Parenting Advice
from a Professional Clown

Kenan Thompson

with Dibs Baer

HARPER

An Imprint of HarperCollins*Publishers*

HarperCollins books may be purchased for educational, business, or sales promotional use. For information, please email the Special Markets Department at SPsales@harpercollins.com.

FIRST EDITION

All photographs courtesy of the author unless otherwise noted.

Designed by Kyle O'Brien

Library of Congress Cataloging-in-Publication Data has been applied for.

ISBN 978-0-06-334806-6

23 24 25 26 27 LBC 5 4 3 2 1

To my entire family, thank you and I love you!

Contents

When I Was
Your Age

PROLOGUE

· · · · · · · · · · · · ·

How long have we known each other? Either you, your kids, or your kids' kids have grown up with me. I've been on your TV or movie screen since I was a kid, more than thirty years now, from *D2: The Mighty Ducks* all the way up to my latest sitcom, *Kenan*. Funny thing is, after all those years, I don't think people know the real me. I guess that's my fault, because most of my life I've been playing crazy characters in kooky costumes on sketch comedy shows like *All That* and *Saturday Night Live*.

Basically, my life comes down to two things: comedy and my family. All I ever wanted to do, as far back as I can remember, was make people laugh like my hero, Eddie Murphy. On *SNL*, I've been smack-dab in the middle of the pop culture zeitgeist every week for twenty years and met every famous (and super famous—what up, Obama?) person on the planet. I'm kind of like Forrest Gump, except I like my shrimp only, like, three ways! At the same time, I'm an uncool dad, stumbling my way through parenting my two little angels, Georgia and Gianna. As I type this, they're nine and five years old. They would much rather be hanging out with their friends than listening to me tell them to keep their elbows off the table or cut down their screen time. They don't even use the word "screen." I feel like a dinosaur using technical words like that. When I text with Georgia, she'll say, "Why do you use so many exclamation points?!" And I say, "Because I'm old!"

I've been through a lot, and now I believe I'm ready to dole out some advice, even if I am not exactly qualified. Hey, you kids, new parents, fellow fathers, budding comics, aunties who want to pinch my cheeks, I got something to say, and maybe you can learn from my biggest mistakes and my most triumphant victories. There's something for everybody here!

I think I have a fresh, funny take on fatherhood, too. Am I doing it right? No idea, but I'm still ready, willing, and able to give my two cents. All I know is I'm doing a lot of things different than my own parents, and sometimes that's good, and sometimes that's not so good.

My parents raised two boys, and I'm raising two girls, so there's a learning curve. My brother, Kerwin, and I were like two peas in a pod. My girls argue a lot more. I have to mediate on the fly. If we're in the car, pretty much the only words I can get out before our destination are "Stop fighting with your sister." I might be able to remind them that, hey, they are sisters, and they should love each other because at the end of the day that sibling bond is the strongest thing on the planet and they need each other, because once their world gets bigger, they'll have to deal with all these other people's nonsense.

My upbringing was just different. Unlike me, my kids can afford a Starter jacket (they're back in style again, a little birdie told me), but they haven't really experienced Black church, which was a huge part of my upbringing. Not sure my dad and his buddies would have ever taken my friends and me to Disney World without the moms and their purses stuffed with supplies for every situation—crayons, snacks, Barbies, clean underwear. A daddy's day out with his daughters to the Magic Kingdom is great on paper but may be more stressful than performing live television! You gotta navigate girls' bathrooms; say no to souvenir stuff every twenty feet; avoid tummy aches after too much sugar stuff. Good luck, parents!

Speaking of, I have two young ladies who will definitely be dealing with body image stuff soon, something I know a lot about, being very publicly known as a big dude. People have been in the news a lot talking about it, and I'll talk about it, too, from a fresh perspective, the Black male point of view. There are some deeper topics in here, like my evolving and ever-changing perspective on race, not only being a Black man but one of the rare, at one time token, Black cast members on *SNL*.

For the *SNL* fans, I've got inspiring advice about the ups and downs of working in showbiz and specifically on that iconic show. I went from playing forgettable bellhops and waiters to winning over the entire Hispanic community with my hungry David Ortiz bit. Don't worry, I've got the juicy stuff, too. I've had so many brushes with the rich (Musk) and infamous (Palin). I've seen a lot of *SNL*'s most legendary cast members, like Andy Samberg, Amy Poehler, and Kristen Wiig, come and go. I've seen Tina Fey rewrite a sketch right before dress rehearsal and rewrite it all again right after. I've shared an office with Colin Jost and worshipped Maya Rudolph.

You guys, my fan base is very diverse. And I'm not just talking about racially, though that's true, too. Fancy research suggests that after me, my fans' favorite celebrities are Chance the Rapper . . . and Bette Midler. Not sure about the wind *beneath* my wings; they probably know more about the wind *after I eat* some wings (insert snort laugh here). One of the stories I love to tell is about the time, back in the early days of *SNL*, Seth Meyers and I had to drive up from NYC to do a stand-up show at University of Rhode Island, but when we got to the car rental place, Seth didn't have a driver's license and I didn't have a credit card. The person behind the counter was not having it, and tippity-typed on her computer annoyed, barely tolerating us with her hateration. We asked to see the manager and an older Black lady came out, instantly recognized me, and smiled from ear to ear.

"Oh! Here you go, baby!" she said sugar sweetly, immediately handing over a set of car keys. "Have fun, fellas!"

I have that sort of genial familiarity. My baby face has always been a blessing and a curse. It definitely makes me super approachable. I'd say I'm like a nice Oodie, cozy and not controversial. I just got a targeted Facebook ad for the Oodie, so it's fresh in my mind. It's basically a rip-off of the Snuggie, but instead of a onesie it's a soft oversized hoodie with different designs on it, like garlic bread or Harry Potter.

Anyhoo, I have a deep connection with my audience. I've been in mainstream fare and/or on network television since 1992, so my brand is extremely family friendly. It's so friendly, people love to come up to me and talk to me about the projects I've done that make them feel nostalgic. Like, the *All That* fans like to freeze me in time, as if I'm still fifteen years old, because maybe that was the best time in *their* life. I'm aight with that! Whatever makes people happy.

It's funny because when people meet me in real life, they expect me to be a goofy-faced jester. I'm actually surprisingly chill. I think I know why. I'm a Black man in America, you know what I'm saying? There's a burden of that life. People want "the show" 24/7, but there's no show. I have a sense of humor. If we speak about things and something funny comes up, we'll laugh and have a good time, but I'm not the guy that needs to be like, "Gather around, everybody!" I'm basically a professional clown for hire. When the nose goes on, I turn on. When the nose comes off, I'm just a regular guy.

• • •

A REGULAR GUY WHO'S HAD A SURREAL LIFE. NOW THAT I'M OLDER (boo) and wiser (yay), and a little jacked—thanks for noticing, I've been working on it—I'm ready to pull the curtain back, tell you some poppin' stories, and impart a little wisdom I've learned along the way. And hopefully make you laugh. Gimme those laughs—that's what I live for!

ONE

······

All That & a Bag of Chips

Growing up a middle-class kid in Georgia, I was a fan of the "off brand." We didn't drink Coke, we drank RC Cola. We didn't eat endless shrimp at Red Lobster, we ate Super Sampler platters at Long John Silver's. We didn't go to Disney World, we went to Six Flags. Gimme Bugs Bunny over Mickey Mouse any day, know what I mean? The Disney Channel? Nah, not yet. Back then I was a huge fan of Nickelodeon, a fledgling cable network for kids whose biggest star was Marc Summers, a hilarious dude in a suit and tie who hosted the game show *Double Dare* and did spot-on Jimmy Stewart and Ethel Merman impressions that flew right over the heads of his pint-sized contestants. I also loved seeing a dude named Phil Moore host *Nick Arcade*. He was so happy-go-lucky, like the kids' version of Al Roker. I got to know him later on, and he's one of the nicest guys in the world. He was never a different person when the cameras weren't rolling. He was always genuine, solid, and supportive. And a little bit nerdy. I love a Black nerd.

I loved how under the radar Nickelodeon was back then, and I loved all their shows, from *You Can't Do That on Television* to that eye-patched little freak known as Danger Mouse. I was a big Nick guy before it was popular. You could tell they were just trying to make their way and figure it out as they went. There was a slapdashy vibe about the whole network, and as an off-brand kind of guy myself, I appreciated that.

So it was pretty surreal the very first day I walked onto the set of *All That*, Nickelodeon's second attempt at a sketch comedy show. *Roundhouse* was the first, an obscure show centered around the "Any-family": everyone looked thirty-two years old, it included high-concept song and dance numbers, and it was (unsuccessfully) sued by Aaron Spelling for relentlessly poking fun at his daughter, Tori. I remember reading in *People* magazine that she had a bowling alley in her basement. I hadn't even known that was possible.

All That was gonna start from scratch, be more straightforward, be more character driven; basically an homage to *Saturday Night Live*, but starring actual kids. I was one of those kids. I was the tender age of fourteen the very monumental day I walked onto the Universal Studios lot in Orlando, Florida. The first thing I saw was Jonathan Brandis's parking spot. At seventeen, he was *the* child star of the moment. He had starred in *Sidekicks*, with Chuck Norris, and *Ladybugs*, with the legendary Rodney Dangerfield. Now he was filming the Steven Spielberg–produced *seaQuest DSV* a few doors down from our set. Jonathan was a hero of mine. I idolized and admired all working child actors because they were #goals. We didn't even know what a hashtag was at that point.

When I first got started in showbiz, there wasn't really one specific project that I wanted to do. I just wanted to be like other kid actors that I saw and knew. I wanted one opportunity to make my stamp. My *Mighty Ducks* buddy Brandon Adams was in *The Sandlot* and *The People Under the Stairs* and played little Michael Jackson in *Moonwalker*. He was prolific. Damn—I mean, sha-mon hee-hee. Another one of my *Mighty Ducks* buddies Aaron Lohr was in *Newsies*, and I thought that was extra extra. Get it? Extra extra. Anyway, he was one out of a hundred kids, but he was *in* the movie. Another guy I looked up to was Dante Basco, who played Rufio in *Hook*. I would have given my real right hand to have been a Lost Boy in *that movie*. David Krumholtz—man, seemed like this kid was in everything. He was in *Life with Mikey* and played Christina Ricci's boyfriend in *Addams Family Values*. He was that kid who worked like a fiend, a go-to for films and commercials, and I envied him in a healthy, positive way. I finally met him about a year ago in a parking garage in New York and he couldn't have been nicer.

To be honest, I wanted to be all of them. A go-to face. The kind everybody knew from a young age as the little dude who had talent. My goal, always, from the beginning, was to start acting, then continue on without stopping or going away. So yeah, seeing Jonathan Brandis's parking spot was like a kids' version of seeing Graceland. I fangirled *out*, inside my head. My first day of *All That* was a day I'll never forget; the memory is very vivid . . . not only because of that first moment you know your life is changing but also because they made us go to school first thing for three hours. How dare you! It wasn't very Hollywood to have to do linear equations at eight a.m. And no, that's not a euphemism for cocaine.

I guess I was the last one in the cast to get picked, because when my mom and I got dropped off at the learnin' trailer right outside our sound stage, everyone already seemed to know one another. I'd just come off filming *D2: The Mighty Ducks*, so I wasn't exactly a rookie, but I was a shy guy in general. I introduced myself then quickly wedged myself into the corner. I admit I was intimidated by my new costars, even ten-year-old Katrina Johnson. There were seven of us, ranging in age from baby Katrina up to seventeen-year-old Lori Beth Denberg.

Lori Beth gave off fierce mama bear energy from day one. She seemed sophisticated, like the old, wise sensei of the bunch, light-years

beyond the rest of us, even though she had the least amount of experience in showbiz. She was damn near an adult already and had this
mature vibe just beaming off her. Women mature faster than men
anyway, so I felt like a little boy next to her. I could tell her vibe was
going to be "older sister having to watch her younger siblings."

The one other Black guy in the room was Kel Mitchell, who was
plucked from a talent search in Chicago. We nodded at each other, you
know, the way "we" do, a quick chin up. Like, *All right, I see you, my
brother.* We had an immediate connection but were still kind of sizing
each other up from a distance. We telepathically communicated with
our eyeballs and chins: *Are you cool? Are you not cool?* When someone's
cool on the Black radar with the head nod and they give it right back
to you, that's perfect. Any deviation from that and it's a problem. You
know we good, and that's all that needs to be said. Like our grandparents probably sharecropped, and everything else under the Black
encyclopedia umbrella is going to align because the struggle is real.
We stick together. If you're Black and you're proud, like James Brown
said, then we're all marching together without having to explain our
beliefs. We all believe that we've been suffering and continue to suffer
and we have an opportunity to carry the torch forward and have a responsibility of elevating the culture and doing it for the ancestors. You
can get all that—pun intended—from just the appropriate timing of a
nod. It's a communal nod.

JOSH SERVER SEEMED COOL WITH EVERYBODY. I LIKED WHITE PEO-
ple. I went to private school for a hot minute, and it had a lot of white
folks, and my gut was telling me from my past experiences with the
whities that Josh was gonna be just fine, even if he didn't season his
food or wash his legs. Time would tell.

There were a couple of ladies, Alisa Reyes and Angelique Bates, and I wondered who was gonna be scheming on these two girls at some point, probably. You know, what's the flavor, neighbor? I could tell Angelique and I were going to be good buddies because she was quirky like me. Alisa was like that meme Little Miss Puerto Rican Spice brought to life. I didn't grow up around any Puerto Ricans, so I was like, *Who is this amazing giraffe walking around?* All of us guys wondered who had a shot, and one of us actually did, but I'm not spilling that tea. It's the '90s kids' version of finding out that Ross and Rachel from *Friends* hooked up. You can't handle the truth!

While the rest of the cast all joked around and talked to each other, I dove into my schoolwork and kept my mouth shut. Everybody was there with their moms, so everybody was behaving themselves, but they did not seem to care about their schoolwork at all. They were all having a great time and not doing their homework. That was the first moment I was like, *Oh, snap, maybe I don't have to be a nerd right now!* Apparently, I was the only nerd. They all seemed so much cooler than me. And different and diverse.

Every once in a while, I'd look up and check out my new cast-mates and get a little side-eye in return. Later on, I learned that everyone thought I had an attitude. There may have been a smidgen of truth to that. When I arrived on *All That*, I was still flying high off making *D2*. The *D2* director, Sam Weisman, knew the creators of *All That*, Brian Robbins and Mike Tollin, and had told them, "You gotta meet this kid," about little ol' me.

I was mad cocky when I went into the audition at NBC offices in LA. I felt I was being handed from one bigwig to the next and already had the job. I didn't even have to wait and scrounge in a hallway with twenty-five other stocky Black dudes who looked exactly like me to be called in front of casting agents. I skipped all that and went straight to producers.

I could tell Brian and Mike were impressed with my confidence.

I was so naïve, I didn't really know that I should be nervous. I might as well have kicked my feet up onto the desk and said, *I heard you guys need my services. I can do whatever you need.* I vaguely remember doing a character with a Jamaican accent on camera. I'm sure there's a tape floating around out there and I'm not as funny as I thought I was. That impression might even get me canceled today, who knows. I wasn't pressed at the time. Even though I was young, I'd already been through the auditioning gauntlet wringer enough to know it was a numbers game. Up to this point it hadn't wrecked my emotions and I didn't take it personally. I remember thinking, *Hey, if this doesn't work out, I'll just head back home to Atlanta and do a Sonic commercial or whatever else comes through. No biggie. It's all good. If they call, they call.*

They called right away.

At first, I was like, *Holy cow, I did it.* But the minute I was sitting in that school trailer, surrounded by so much fresh talent, all the nerves hit me. My castmates mistook my paralyzing fear for "attitude." This was my first TV gig. Who the *H-E*–double hockey sticks did I think I was? Ignorance had been bliss. Now this was really happening, and I was kind of sharting my pants. This TV thing was a whole different approach. Did I even know what I was doing? I did. I had to remind myself I was a legit actor and had a bunch of decent credits under my belt.

I'd never done zany characters yet per se, but my older brother, Kerwin, and I were big fans of sketch comedy growing up. My love for performance started with my brother for sure. We watched *In Living Color* and all the shows and films in the Black zeitgeist, from *I'm Gonna Git You Sucka* to *Hollywood Shuffle*. All the Eddie Murphy bits on *SNL*, and his comedy specials and movies. This was before cell phones and iPads, so on eight-hour road trips from Atlanta to Virginia, where our extended family lived, we were bored as all get-out. It ain't easy to color in the car; you just can't do it, as hard as you try. You can only ask truck drivers to honk their horns so many times. Punch Buggy is fun for about twenty minutes. To pass the time, Kerwin and I would requote movies beginning to end. *Coming to America* and *Three Amigos!* were our favorites. There were a lot of characters in both, so we naturally did a lot of tone and accent work performing them to each other in the back seat.

"Good morning, my neighbors!"

"Hey, fuck you!"

"Yes, yes. Fuck you, too!"

We were so silly together. We would clown each other and say, "Nah, that ain't it, we gotta do it better." Practicing over and over organically led to doing good impressions. Eventually, we sounded just like the scene in the movie.

Before the Internet, we watched the same cable TV stuff millions of times. That's what kids did back then. *Smokey and the Bandit*, all the John Hughes movies, *The Princess Bride*, *Spies Like Us*, *Young Guns* both I and II. Which came in handy later for one of my most famous sketch comedy bits on *SNL*, "Scared Straight," in which my prison mentor character, Lorenzo McIntosh, screams the plots of '80s movies at wayward teens. That was pretty much my experience doing broad characters up to that point.

When I was sitting in that sterile *All That* classroom, I could feel my self-esteem disintegrating by the minute. I didn't shake out of it until eleven a.m., when we were finally taken to the studio for the first time. When we walked onto the sound stage, the set was a playground. I saw a legit jungle gym and a basketball hoop, and my heart soared. It was ours, you know what I mean? Just the seven of us. It belonged to us, nobody else.

It was time to read scripts and perform. During that first rehearsal, we all played three peewee sports together and got to show off our skills. I was a decent athlete, having played peewee football until my child acting took priority. I channeled my inner MJ and kept making so many shots, like eight in a row. I officially earned my dude props from that.

Now it was time to show off my comedy skills. I remember wanting to make Lori Beth laugh, because if you did, it meant you were smart enough. It always felt complimentary when you could get a laugh out of Lori Beth. We filmed the pilot, and I was definitely one of the go-tos from the jump. It was clear that when the higher-ups wanted to figure out a character or a sketch, they were like, "Let Kenan try it." That felt good. And it felt good when my peers got to see that I was funny. From then on, it was gravy.

Everyone was so talented. The pilot had some classic sketches, like "Glorp," our take on *The Blob*, where ooze takes over our minds and makes us brainless. In "Cool Shoes," we all kept leveling up our sneakers, like it started with air cushions, the next one had a water gun on it, and finally an ice cream dispenser. The very first episode also unleashed "Good Burger" on the world. The sketch, about a fast-food cashier named Ed who always messes stuff up, was specifically created for Kel. He was one of the few in the cast to have a whole sketch to himself. I didn't at that point, and in the early episodes in "Good Burger," I played "Lester Oaks, construction worker." For some reason, construction workers always sounded country to me instead of New Yorky. I chose to do a Southern accent, maybe because of my good ol' Georgia upbringing or maybe I was watching *Urban Cowboy* and *Smokey and the Bandit* a lot at that time. I dunno. I do know I had a lot of fun with that character, Lester Oaks, construction worker.

But "Good Burger" was Kel's jam. I remember watching him do his thing and thinking, *This dude's a powerhouse,* 'cause he just ran with it. I could easily have been jealous of Kel in that moment, but I instinctively understood that there was room for all of us to shine on this show. Kel and I organically clicked for the first time when we performed

"Mavis & Clavis" together, playing two old Black men. I was from the South Side of Atlanta, and Kel was from the South Side of Chicago, so we'd both witnessed old Black men jawing a million times. Kel and I made each other laugh, and that's when we really bonded. Then we started talking and realized we had so many eerily similar experiences growing up. We were kind of the same person. Raised by parents who grew up in the '50s. From segregated cities. Grew up in the theater. Kel was very artistic and wrote a lot of poetry, but our one difference is that he was much more political than me. This was way before I grew into my consciousness. In Chicago, they were militant about the assassination of Black Panther Fred Hampton in a police raid. In my pocket of Atlanta, we celebrated the peacefulness of Martin Luther King Jr., and turned the cheek a little bit.

Josh was from Chicago as well. He actually had his own pilot on Nickelodeon right before *All That*, but it didn't get picked up. Didn't matter, I gave him his props, he was basically a star in my eyes already. I don't know why, but Josh and I were on a different vibe, and he is one of my closest friends to this day. He just matched my energy. Maybe because I'm a Taurus and he's an Aries, right on the cusp? Don't ask me why or how I know anything about that astrology stuff, I just do.

Kel and I were thrown together a lot from the start for obvious, some may say cynical, reasons. We were both Black, duh. I mean, usually a show like that would have one token Black guy, but *All That* had two. It was kind of groundbreaking and prolific; you hadn't seen a young Black duo becoming a Laurel and Hardy or Martin and Lewis. There were young Black guys on shows together, like Todd Bridges and Gary Coleman on *Diff'rent Strokes* and Will Smith and Alfonso Ribeiro on *The Fresh Prince of Bel-Air*.

Our pairing was kismet, too. I believe it was meant to happen. Kel became my brother. He was very much down with the Black zeitgeist, which was fine, because I had all that info, too, but he wasn't trying to talk about *Best in Show* or *Raising Arizona* with Josh and me. Just wasn't his thing. But we had a deep connection. Whenever my mom went back to Atlanta to work, I stayed with Kel's family at their place. His parents were still together, and they were very warm and inviting. His little sister was a baby, and we put her in the "Bagging Sagging Barry" sketch. I had these sagging pants that carried anything I needed, from a lantern to a two-liter bottle of soda. At some point, I pulled his baby sister outta my pants for no reason. So she got a cameo.

Kel, Josh, and I became the Three Amigos. We had a plethora of piñatas and felt like we were the captains of the SS *All That*. Lori Beth was the queen, of course. But whenever the writers needed something, who did they turn to? The three sons of a motherless goat. From very early on, and for the next five years, us three boys were inseparable. We loved the girls, but we were kind of separated from them, probably to make sure we weren't humping around all day. Even still, we were just on a different page than our female costars. They were too young for us—we were looking for Halle Berry, basically.

The girls needed to be protected with so many random people on set; they couldn't just be wandering around by themselves. But the boys? You could just open the door and tell 'em to come back later. And that's exactly what happened. The Three Amigos discovered one little side gate where we could just walk right into the Universal theme park. Every day on our lunch break, we grabbed a hamburger from the commissary, rolled out of our studio, ran past Jonathan Brandis's parking spot and paid our respects (we never saw him once; he was like a unicorn), then snuck into what can only be described as heaven for teenage boys. We weren't famous yet, so we could wander around anonymously. We rode King Kong and Terminator 2: 3D too many times to count. It was epic.

The powers that be started to catch on after we snuck a bunch of girls into Halloween Horror Nights and left a gate open. At first, everyone was invited to come on our adventures, but we were forced to get a little more exclusive after, I believe, Katrina's parents got suspicious and asked, "Where were you guys?" after one extra-long lunch escapade. Katrina was forbidden to go, but that wasn't about to stop the Three Amigos. As soon as we punched out for lunch, we ran around the corner, and we were free. We were happy kids. We felt like kings!

The three of us got into all sorts of teenage hijinks. No, we weren't out there robbing tourists or threatening to harm the Mickey Mouse Club (though for the record, I did think Kel could take Ryan Gosling). Just some regular teenager stuff. I could Rollerblade pretty well after *D2*, so while Kel and Josh would try to pick up chicks at the mall, I'd skate around in an attempt to show them up. It never worked. I had my driver's license, but no car. That didn't stop me from making like any normal teenager and borrowing my mom's rental car for the very important purpose of doing donuts in the Publix parking lot.

It's not like we ever did anything unsafe, unless you count riding Back to the Future so many times you puke up a little hamburger in your mouth. Many an afternoon was spent riding the DeLorean or yelling at King Kong before heading back to set. Every Halloween we'd sneak friends in and laugh at the lanky teenager in the Michael Myers mask. I mean, it's not like we snuck off to our biggest competitor, Disney World. Bite your tongue! The one time I did go to our rival, the Nickelodeon gods were not happy. I saw my first concert, the Isley Brothers, in Downtown Disney. It was an outdoor theater, but the stage was elevated. Everybody was crammed below, on the same plane. I was much shorter than the crowd, and I found myself stuck in the middle of the scrum. I got all dizzy and knew I was about to pass out. I tried to get out to the edge, but it was like Nemo and Dory making their way through the jellyfish in *Finding Nemo*. I couldn't breathe and thought, *Holy moly, man, I'm losing oxygen from being surrounded by a bunch of butts.*

I didn't die, luckily, but how embarrassing if:

1. I lost my life at an Isley Brothers concert. Nothing cool about that.
2. I lost my life because I was short.

Needless to say, I stuck faithfully to our Nickelodeon/Universal campus after that, where my friendship with Kel and Josh blossomed into something special, spiritual, iconic. Those guys helped me break out of my shell, and I am forever indebted to them for that. We loved the fact that we were all actors. That we all had a job, a real gig. Being a part of the Three Amigos helped me understand that I was where I belonged, doing what I was meant to do. Delivering laughs to these kids watching Nickelodeon, running around with each other, and having the time of our lives. We soaked it all up, knowing and loving that we'd be back again early the next morning. We never wanted to let it go.

TWO

Back in the Day

For my daughter Gianna's fourth birthday, we did something really special. I took my kids to my hometown of Atlanta and stayed at an Airbnb in my neighborhood instead of a hotel downtown. I alternately bored them silly and surprised them, telling them stories about my childhood: How I never had an iPhone or any of those fancy things kids these days have. I had to play with cigarette butts!

Now that I'm a dad, I want my girls to have a lot of the same things I had growing up, but then there's obviously going to be some very different things. Like, I grew up middle-class-ish in an all-Black-ish neighborhood, just outside Atlanta's main drag, Interstate 285, aka the Perimeter Highway, a beltway loop that encircles the city. Where I'm from, the vibe inside the circle was pretty different from the vibe outside the circle. My family lived inside the circle, in the pocket of old Black Atlanta, closer to downtown. We lived minutes from the airport, so yeah, it was noisy.

We weren't necessarily poor, but we definitely weren't rich. We ate at home a lot, and Red Lobster was a big deal. I don't think we traveled too much; we didn't hit the beaches in Florida every summer. We might have gone to New York once? There wasn't a Mercedes in the neighborhood; everybody had a pickup truck or a Toyota. We only drove Hondas, and never wore Jordans or Starter jackets. All the adults worked a lot. We went to friends' houses for card games, and we were church people. That took up all of our time, and we were fine with that.

Before the Olympics came in 1996, Atlanta was still a small town, basically Columbus, Ohio, with a twang. I loved all the good-not-evil Southern things about Atlanta, like soul food and weeping willows and iced tea and fans. Even though I lived in an urban metropolis, I very much felt Southern, but more country bumpkin than, say, *Woo, Lord, it's so hot out here! I would love some lemonade!* Everyone I knew, all of my friends' parents or somebody near their generation, came from a farm setting and probably had sharecropping or picking cotton in their family histories.

My extended family originally came from Virginia. My mom, Elizabeth—she goes by her middle name, Ann—grew up in the woods of Bedford, on a forty-acres-and-a-mule gifted property, the first land that they were able to get post-emancipation. And they stayed on that land. We're talking very, very humble beginnings. A bunch-of-people-in-one-room type thing. My dad, Fletcher, grew up in downtown Lynchburg but still only had an outhouse outside his home. "Wow, you lived in a city that has buses and stuff but still didn't have indoor plumbing?" I asked him. It used to terrify him to use the outhouse—it was freezing and pitch-black in the winter, and in the summer he had to look for snakes before he drained the lizard. That really bugged me out. It felt like that should have been *his* father's upbringing. Was it the 1800s or the 1950s? This hit too close to home.

My parents met at the downtown Lynchburg hospital where my mom worked as a nurse. My dad came in with his brother after they got in a bar fight (not coincidentally, my dad's nickname was "Wine"). After getting married and having my older brother, Kerwin, and me, my parents moved to Atlanta for more opportunity, but the city was extremely segregated at the time. It was either Black or white and not much else. No Mexican, Indian, Asian. It wasn't a melting pot like that. Atlanta was the definition of the "Jim Crow South."

I vividly remember, whenever we took road trips to see our family in Virginia, my dad always brought his gun. I always wondered what he expected to run into. Early on, I was pretty unaware of the civil rights struggle that had happened right under my nose in Atlanta, even though the spirit of Martin Luther King Jr. was everywhere. He grew up there; his father's church, Ebenezer Baptist, was there; and the King Center was there. But I didn't have a real awakening about racism, systemic inequality, and all of that until high school.

I don't think my parents shielded me from it. It wasn't readily apparent. Where I came from, everybody kicked it with their own people. Our family hangs out with our family, and your family hangs out with your family. Because, even amongst us, we had beef with the kids up the street, and they were Black. They weren't our family, and I didn't really know them. If my cousin said we got beef, then we got beef.

As a young boy, I filmed a fried chicken commercial that was blatantly racist, and I remember thinking to myself, *Is this racist?* but an old Black man in it with me didn't seem to mind, so I thought it was okay. The first time I drove with friends through a ritzy neighborhood, within a few seconds cops were following closely behind, as if these four drama dorks, who happened to be Black, were going to stir up some trouble in my mom's avocado-green-and-tan Accord. It was the first time I became conscious of the experience of the adult Black male, and I was only sixteen. Others aren't so lucky. I got profiled and pulled over several times, including once with Kel, but was always let go. For me, overt racism hadn't become a reality yet.

In eleventh grade, all of the dots finally connected. I was aware of oppression and civil rights and slavery, but I hadn't been aware of the systemic version of it or that prison was basically modern-day slavery. I had an awakening, and I remember telling my mom and her just listening to me, letting me get it out without interrupting or arguing, because everything I was saying was true. I'll never forget the sadness in her eyes when she saw my loss of innocence. It's a sad day when you have to discuss the unfairness that's been established in this country.

But Atlanta felt very Black and white growing up, and I was happily existing in my bubble. When we did mix, everyday conversations often felt like a chatter across cultures as opposed to just two people talking. Whenever my dad would introduce somebody that he worked with who was white, all of a sudden it was this different voice and energy. He didn't do this toward his friends. That could have been a race thing. That could have been a professional thing. It wasn't quite as extreme as a *yessa, boss* kind of thing, but it was a little bit of that. "This is Mr. Smith, and him and his kids are real good people."

That was stuff on the surface; I hadn't really done an in-depth study on it. And it's not like anyone was going out of their way to teach this type of stuff. As I got older, I had my awakening. It was shocking because it was so pointed at me by people that I had never even met. Yet they had made all these decisions about the possibilities of my life without giving me a chance. Things are built into the system to keep you under a certain kind of glass ceiling. I had spent sixteen years thinking the sky was the limit. We could do anything.

I came to realize that my dad brought a loaded gun on our family trips because he was planning on running into racists. Maybe the-middle-of-nowhere-nobody's-looking kind of racists. Especially driving through the Carolinas to Virginia, know what I mean? That's a whole lot of Dixie territory to be trucking through just to see Grandma. But we had to do it, especially because all I wanted to do was eat my grandmother's food. Everything she made was incredible; her oatmeal and scrambled eggs were *oh lordy*–worthy. She also made the most phenomenal fried bologna sandwiches with lettuce, tomato, mayo, and salt and pepper on white bread. I wanted them every day. She was one of those people that could make a plain-ass sandwich taste great. I used to love ripping off that little red strip off the edge of the bologna and nibbling on the leftover meat inside the strip before I threw it away.

As the patriarch, my dad was prepared to protect his family on a trip through the sticks. I don't have a deadly weapon in my car to protect my girls, Gianna and Georgia; I have mini flat-screen TVs in the headrests playing *SpongeBob SquarePants*. It's not that I necessarily grew up softer than my dad, just different.

It's not an easy conversation—talking about race—to have to have with your child, but it's one I will have to have with my girls. The irony is that I ended up on *SNL*, a show that didn't do a good job not being obvious about its own systemic racism. For so long they were so far behind, and I was angry that I was the token Black guy trying to figure out a way to punch through. At the same time, I felt very spoiled. I was getting a dose of how much privilege I was eating up on a daily basis, without even thinking twice about it. I was aware of the struggle being real because some of my family in Virginia used to have old houses that were grandfathered to them, but they had construction lights in the living room and couldn't afford heat. I just wasn't aware of how almost impenetrable the struggle would continue to be.

MY BROTHER, KERWIN, AND I WERE CITY KIDS, AND COLLEGE PARK, or as we all called it, "Colle'Pawk," which proudly harbors the world's busiest airport several years running, was our original stomping ground. Atlanta back then was definitely Black Mecca. It had swag and its very own Southern pride, and our sports teams had a flavor, especially the HBCUs (historically Black colleges and universities).

Atlanta's ugly racial history is deep and long, and now we were on the other side of it, trying to swim in the other direction, and Atlanta was like, *Yeah, we know that's our past, but this is what we're trying to do with our future.* That was the vibe when I was growing up. We listened to rap music and drove downtown and caused all kinds of traffic issues to party in the street. It was all Black, and it's where Ludacris had his radio show—shout-out to his cohost, Poon Daddy—which made it cool. That was my era.

Not so cool is that I grew up two minutes from the airport. Take-offs and landings were the soundtrack to my upbringing, 'cause we were right under all the landing patterns. It was always rattling our crib, all these super-loud planes flying over our heads. Despite the cacophony of jet engines, College Park had real charm, it looked like a neighborhood, and it had beautiful old trees. As opposed to those carved-out communities where every house looked the same and there were no trees because they chopped them all down to make room for the McMansions.

When I was eleven-ish, my mom wanted to move to a better neighborhood, so ultimately, we migrated down the same street, called Old National Highway, to right outside the 285 loop, to one of those cookie-cutter subdivisions in Southwest Atlanta, aka the SWATS.

Atlanta felt so free back in my day. We were such latchkey kids. The adults worked 24/7, so we got ourselves up in the morning, fixed our own cereal, and watched a prime-time-worthy lineup of cartoons back-to-back. Your *He-Man* would be on, followed by *Transformers*, which would be followed by *Thundercats*, followed by *Ninja Turtles*. It was action-packed! We didn't need coffee to wake up; we had adrenaline from the misogyny of *G.I. Joe*, the violence of *Tom & Jerry*, and the horniness from the missiles coming out of the female robot's boobs on *Tranzor Z*.

On the weekends, our parents wanted to sleep in and not be

bothered, so they let us run amok from sunrise 'til sunset, even after an estimated twenty-seven Black children were kidnapped and murdered in Atlanta, allegedly by convicted murderer Wayne Williams between 1979 and 1981. One time my brother accidentally got left at school during that era. My poor mom had a really terrible afternoon, and the cops brought Kerwin home later that night. I don't remember the panic, but they tell the story with fear still to this day.

When I was about nine, my mom started letting me take the train by myself downtown to the theater. It went straight there; she knew I was a smart cookie, and there was no way I could mess it up. If you put a kid alone on a train today, somebody would film it on their iPhone, post it on TikTok to the Sarah McLachlan animal cruelty song, and it'd go viral, there'd be public outcry.

For the most part, as long as we were back in time for dinner, the vibe from our exhausted parents back in the day was roam if you want to. Especially if it was Saturday morning. They were basically like, "Just get out of our hair, have a great weekend." We came back when we were hungry or hurt or the streetlights came on. Of course, they had a vague sense of where we were because we all hung out at each other's houses. This was before Nintendo. Maybe one person on our block had Atari at this point. They knew this one particular kid's backyard was for baseball and my other buddy's driveway was good for basketball. Maybe the parents were calling each other to keep tabs, but I doubt it.

MY MOM WAS STRICT. SHE IS THE OLDEST OF SEVEN, SO SHE'S A leader. She's also very highly organized, the perfect storm of a Pisces. My mom took life seriously. Anytime you heard all of your names, you knew you were in trouble. She'd yell commands at me like, "Kenan

Stacy Thompson, you need to wear a belt," or "Kenan Stacy Thompson, breathe oxygen!" She was big on manners and reading and writing. She was in a monthly book club long before Oprah owned that scene. My mom made sure we spoke properly and did our homework. Our education: she was all over it.

My mom has an infectious smile. A lot of times, it was a smiling-through-the-pain kind of smile that comes when you struggle economically. If she was dealing with a lot, you couldn't really tell she was. She was able to carry a lot on her shoulders without whining about it the whole time. She's kind of unflappable. She doesn't take no mess. My mom was my be-all and end-all. She was the first person I was looking for in the morning and the last person to tuck us in at night. She was the one that guided us through what we needed to know about life.

My mom has since moved, but our old house was still there when I drove by with my girls, so I took a picture of it. It was so fun to see everything kinda still frozen in time, even as I slowly and painfully discovered that my babies didn't give a hoot about my trip down memory lane. "Hey, that's the soul food place where we would always go after church!" I'd say, pointing at historic restaurant the Beautiful, amazed that it was still there. My dad used to love their breakfast, so we would go before church, after church, and for any kind of celebration of any sort. It was my favorite, too, and all the people who worked there were so friendly. It was a small place beloved by the locals. It was known for its biscuits, catfish, ham hocks, and ribs. Martin Luther King Jr. ate there once allegedly supposedly, and it was known as a safe haven for people protesting during the civil rights era.

Anyway, Gianna and Georgia couldn't care less about the Beautiful or anything else we drove by, like my school. I don't blame them. Basically, they were looking at buildings. "You see that big, giant house?" I'd ask no one in particular. "It used to be just a shack. Then they built a giant house around it because they finally came into some money. Look at that super-duper-modern McMansion," I clucked. "If you know the original frame, you can still see the front door."

My lecture about suburban sprawl couldn't really compete with petting a stingray at the Georgia Aquarium or receiving a free refreshing soft drink after a tour at World of Coca-Cola. I was just talking out the window about real estate, just like my own pops.

My dad was the disciplinarian. He had to go to work, so there was no time for his kids to be giving him a headache. If you were annoying him, you were gonna get a whooping. He had no time to be dealing with foolishness. He was a Vietnam veteran, a helicopter mechanic in the army. He wasn't in the killing fields, but he was involved in it. He could fix anything.

My dad was the kind of guy who was good at whatever he took on, a jack-of-all-trades. Before I was born, he got to experience Europe without a whole lot of oppression attached to it. He drove race cars and was in a band. He even cut an album and met Jimi Hendrix. When I was a kid, he got his real estate license and was killing it so hard as an agent at Century 21, he got one of those fancy gold jackets—you know, the ones that kinda made them all look like they were hosting *Family Feud* in the Richard Dawson era. My dad had the best personality; he was a joke teller who would tell people to "gather round." He could make my strictest grandma almost pee her pants laughing. He enjoyed a cocktail or two, and as I mentioned, his nickname was "Wine," which is where my brother gets his middle name, "Vino," from.

Now would be a good time to tell you more about Kerwin, who is four years older than me. Ever since I could walk, I followed him everywhere. "You never leave Kenan behind," my mom instructed to him. "You do not go anywhere and leave him alone. You're the big brother. Big brothers have responsibilities." I was jealous of everything about my brother, down to his middle name. My parents gave me the corniest middle name of them all, Stacy. I played that one close to the vest until the Atlanta Hawks drafted Stacey Augmon in '91. That dude did more for the name Stacy/ey than I ever could. I'm also pretty sure he's one of my cousins from Virginia—at least that's what I told everyone back home.

Firstborns, like Kerwin, are the jewels of their parents' eyes. They're the first to do everything, the ones who should know better, and he was the one I was supposed to listen to, because he knew more than I did because he'd been here longer, basically. But he was opinionated and rebellious to the point that when he would chaperone me on jobs sometimes, my mom would say to me, "Now, don't let Kerwin get into trouble." He was always so much smarter than me. We did everything boys do, watched cartoons, played sports. We used to play football on our block, two-hand touch in the street, but violent sideline tackles into the grass were absolutely allowed and encouraged. We rode our bikes everywhere. I had a BMX, and my brother had a banana seat bike. I rode it one time and wrecked it because this kid was on the back with me, and he panicked and wobbled and made me wipe out. To this day, my fingernail is split down the middle and has a little Quasimodo hump.

KERWIN AND I WENT HAND IN HAND THROUGH LIFE TOGETHER. I feel like we spent more time together than with our parents. It's such a different time now. So many parents hang out with their kids like they're best friends. But no way in bejesus I'd let my girls wander around all day by themselves, hand in hand or otherwise. And I certainly wouldn't let them jump off the second-story staircase in their grandma's house, like I did with my brother and my cousin Tre. We were always trying to jump as high and as far as we could, basically almost tearing down the front entryway. When we were acting up over at her house, Grandma would make us pick out our own switch from the yard then pull the leaves and twigs off ourselves before we got whacked. That was the worst process ever.

I only caught a couple switches for being rambunctious—you know, slamming doors and running in and out of the house and not listening. You can't spank without a visit from social services nowadays, though there are some deep red school districts trying to bring back corporal punishment. But I really don't believe in hitting kids at all; it's not effective. Even if you just pop them on the leg, that can be traumatic. What I've learned is I have to be persistent anytime I disagree with behavior that is not acceptable. Push it to the limit until they understand and change their behavior. Whether it's a time-out or a "Go sit in your room and think about what you did." They know I'm not playing. Otherwise, you're going to raise a kid who's gonna butt heads into something that could get them suspended or worse. As you get older, the consequences of acting out are more dire, especially as a Black person in America, and I would hate for my kids to think they're invincible until they ran up against the police.

It felt so good to point out to Gianna and Georgia where I fell off my bike, got pantsed, broke my first bone, whether they caught the sentimentality or not. Do kids get broken bones anymore nowadays? With all this newfangled helicopter parenting? The only helicopter I saw as a kid was when the local weatherman choppered onto our school playground, then performed a puppet show that explained the different types of clouds. As if the helicopter wasn't enough, you have to do a puppet show, too? Atlanta was so loose back then, it was a smaller market and still the Wild West. Nowadays, can you imagine the red tape of trying to get permission to land a helicopter on an elementary school playground?

• • •

THE ONLY THING I'M A PUSHOVER ABOUT IS ROBLOX. GEORGIA'S constantly hitting me up for Robux. I try to make her see that she's spending all this money on nothing, but she hasn't connected the dots. All her friends are on there chatting. It's crazy.

I'm proud that Georgia and Gianna are well-behaved young ladies. Usually. Though they bicker a little over sharing toys or snacks. I give my girls Cheerios, just like my mama gave Kerwin and me, because I think it's so cute that kids love them. But when they fight over said Cheerios on our road trip, I'm not gonna lie, I definitely channeled my mom a few times, yelling, "Apparently, you don't want to go where we're going! I will turn this car right around and we will go straight home and we're not gonna see Grandma!" I never thought I'd be that person. But sometimes "I will turn this car around" is all you have in your arsenal.

All in all, my girls are little angels, especially because I play the counting game to 100 and they'll fall asleep by like 47. That probably won't work when they're older, but I have high hopes that when they're thirteen, they'll still be Daddy's little sweethearts while everyone else's preteens are monsters. Being good is in their DNA, I hope. I wasn't a fire starter. I was a pretty good boy and very "agreeable," my mom tells me. That's more a credit to my parents. Both of them were trying to raise good upstanding Black men. We knew we were Black; we knew the importance—it was hammered into us—that we be upstanding Black men out in the world. We had that in mind when we were around an unfamiliar situation. We knew we were in the South. We were surrounded by people that looked like us, listened to the same music, watched the same shows. It was a very one-sided environment for sure, and I admit I loved every second of it.

Georgia and Gianna are experiencing a much more diverse upbringing than I had. They're deeply submerged in the melting pot, surrounded by every color of the rainbow, especially living and going to school in New York City. So far, race hasn't come up. You know what has? LGBTQ+ issues, because they go to school in the West Village. They're already learning about embracing other people's lifestyles. But not race yet. I don't think they're overly aware of culture at the moment. I make sure they have Black dolls, that their toys represent what they see in the mirror, but I don't know if they understand the classification that society has already put them in. Once that happens, their innocence is gone forever; they're aware of the establishment, the system. There's no turning back.

It's important my daughters develop that connection because it'll guide the rest of their lives. My own upbringing—especially my mom and dad and my neighborhood—has guided me as a parent. My dad taught me to be a patriarch and provider.

When I was twelve, my parents got divorced. It didn't affect my upbringing 'cause I think I was already pretty much up, but it definitely wasn't great. Like there's nothing happy or anything to celebrate about it. The only positive I think that came from it was probably my half sister, Feleecia, and her side of the family. She's my half sister but my whole heart! They're all very sweet people. Besides that, it was just weird. It was weird to watch my mom date people, and it was weird to watch my dad get remarried. It was a blanket of weird over any kind of positive aspects I could have taken away from it.

All of a sudden, it seemed like nobody was around anymore. My dad was gone. I wasn't home that much. My mom was not home that much. My brother was with friends then off to college. I was spending my time with myself alone or a friend across the street. Shout-out to Weldon! Luckily, I was already known for being a kid who could entertain himself pretty well. It taught me that. I'll be fine if I have to go out in the world and spend a whole lot of time with myself, like I'll probably be okay.

My parents' split was hard on all of us but especially my dad because he was no longer the provider and protector of his family. It had a big effect on me later on down the road, especially when I became a father and put it all into perspective.

My dad was a rock star in so many different directions—musician, mechanic, real estate legend—and I remember wanting to be half as cool as him. Basically, what happened was after my dad left the corporate real estate world to open his own business, he ran smack into that discrimination nonsense, where the white powers that be were trying to say that he could only show certain listings. He ended up being on the front lines of the fight for any real estate agent being able to show any listing, like in the history of the state of Georgia. He got death threats constantly. It ruined his practice, and he was basically run out of the real estate business.

This is all documented, and he very recently was officially recognized for his role in fighting discrimination in the real estate world. Too little, too late. Life spiraled out of control for him. The stress caused my parents' divorce and just drained that spirit out of him. He was never quite the same, to be honest. We all witnessed him bear the burden of putting his business and his whole family's future on the line for the sake of what was right. I always knew he was a smart man and capable of a lot. I saw him doing well at Century 21, but as soon as he opened his own business—I was still in like third or fourth grade—everything spun out of control. We just always prayed for him.

I'm grateful for that lesson my dad's experience taught: always fight for what's right, no matter the outcome. You have to make a decision and be prepared for the worst. I'm sure my father contemplated: *Do I make change and sacrifice my business and my family's financial future, opportunity, and safety? Or do I sit back knowing that this isn't right in my heart just to watch my yard and not really make any specific progress for others?* I watched him put his personal fears aside for the betterment of others. I didn't know that until much later, but I watched the fallout of the situation not really knowing the whole story. Once I found that out, I realized it was a very brave, bold choice. I thought that was a very stand-up lesson. He sacrificed a lot, because his life was night and day from that point on.

I'm also grateful for the personality traits I inherited from my dad. We both have that gung ho personality. We can stand in any crowd and survive. I'm a bit of a jack-of-all-trades, too, which came in handy when playing different kinds of characters on *All That* and *SNL*. Like, we had a pool table in the basement and my dad was a bit of a shark, and I've got a little bit of that skill, too. He was a joke teller, and I'm a professional clown. Actually, I think my sense of humor is a blend of the two of them. Because my mom loves to laugh, too, but she's kind of prissy.

The biggest lesson I got from my parents was the importance of being present. Both my mom and dad were very present throughout my childhood. I never felt alienated or that I didn't have anyone to call in case of a crisis. I always felt protected. But let's not get it twisted: my parents did not baby us. They were strict, and I think I learned that I was kind of being a little too strict with my daughters and not necessarily identifying with the emotional processing of certain disciplinary moments. I used to be all about the "Because I said so . . ." or if Georgia or Gianna were upset, my knee-jerk reaction was to say, "Quit crying!" because that's what my brother and I got growing up. I've come to realize that's not helpful when you're raising girls. They deserve a sweet, the-magic-is-real aspect of childhood. They deserve to be able to hold on to that as long as possible.

I do my best not to spoil my kids, even though they have a lot more than I had growing up. I took Georgia to a live taping of *America's Got Talent*. I don't do stuff like that often. I told her, "I'm only doing this because it's your favorite show." And I had an in with Tape Face.

I'm always checking myself by asking, *How much is too much?* Maybe it's because I saw plenty of poverty in Atlanta before being blessed enough to drink expensive wines with Hollywood A-listers. I try to teach my girls to appreciate what we have, keep their rooms in order, and do their homework. If they want the new toy of the month, I make sure they understand they're lucky I'm able to afford it. Parenting is like 50 percent mind games and 50 percent Amazon orders. You win, Bezos.

THREE

Tuesday Is a Church Day, Too!

When I lived under my mother's roof, every Sunday morning I woke up to the velvety voices of gospel duo CeCe and BeBe Winans praising Jesus. Which may sound heavenly but, in reality, was hell. Especially when it's seven a.m., you're an exhausted teenager, and you much prefer the sonic funk of Outkast. My mom wanted our butts out of bed for church, so at the crack of dawn, she blasted Black gospel music at the highest level the dB scale allows for human eardrums. Fortunately for my mom, and unfortunately for my brother and me, when we moved, our new house had an intercom system. So when "Well, Alright" rang throughout every room of the house, it was so loud, it was impossible to keep sleeping. Believe me, I tried holding my ears, covering my head with a pillow—man, nothing could drown out CeCe and Bebe's devotion.

This was not a game. My mom was not playing—not going to church was not an option, nor was it a topic up for discussion. Sure, there was one year we attempted to fight back . . . annnd we lost. Wasn't close. After that, she stopped even mentioning the fact that it was Sunday; we were just supposed to know. When that gospel came on, the silent but deadly serious message was, *Y'all know if you don't get up and get in the car, it's gonna be a problem.*

Once the Winans shook me out of my REM sleep, I would eventually drag my sorry butt outta bed. But then I remembered I had a church crush and the thought of seeing that cutie motivated me to get moving. I always wanted to impress this particular young lady, so I made sure I smelled good—a shower and a little splash of Drakkar Noir—and looked nice and spiffy. I'm having visions of vests. Lots and lots of vests. A suit is one thing, but when you add that vest, now you're trying to be distinguished. Vest and tie make the man. It's a hard thing to stand out amongst millions, so a vest is not necessarily a bad starting place, as far as individual character development.

Church was my whole life. TVs only had a few channels back in the day, and preachers like Jimmy Swaggart and Tammy Faye Bakker had a strong hold on the programming in my house. There was another old man with silver hair who was always praying. He was hunched over and never opened his eyes. I watched him get older and older in that same position. The Bible thumping was especially heavy on the holidays. Every Christmas, we watched all 220 minutes of the 1956 classic *The Ten Commandments*, starring Charlton Heston as Moses. It was really, really long. By hour three, I was hoping a divine intervention or a plague would liberate *me* and let me go to bed so Santa could come to our house and leave lots of presents.

Home was about church, school was about church. I went to a Christian academy for grade school, and they programmed that Bible learning into our heads right along with our ABCs. We did the Pledge of Allegiance first, sang "Onward, Christian Soldiers," then started school. They set the religious agenda first thing in the morning, then throughout the day, there was lots of scripture reading. My favorite sword drill was called Knowing Your Bible, where a teacher calls out a random verse, like "Hebrews 13:12!" and you're supposed to be the first one to find it, wherever it is. I was competitive. I knew it had something to do with blood and Jesus's haters making him suffer. I flipped through my King James like a maniac. "I got it!" I yelled out. Then I got to read it. That was the prize, reading it. Was it more fun than Heads Up, 7-Up on a rainy day with no recess? Getting your thumb pressed down by a cute girl was pretty sweet. But I was tight with this drill. I knew the Bible and the Books because I had a pretty good memory. That came in handy then and was good practice for later in life when I had to memorize scripts.

I was all about that church life. Not many Black folks I know can't relate. Church is one of the major backbones of Black culture, especially Southern Black culture, for sure. It's built-in. The attitude where I came from was, if you didn't grow up going to church five times a week, then you didn't know nothing. In my single digits, I went to church a lot. Did I say "a lot"? I meant "all the time." We could be visiting my grandma in Virginia, and she'd tell us to get our lazy butts down to her church, Diamond Hill Baptist, even if it was a Tuesday afternoon and we didn't know a soul there. In the summertime we went nearly every day, just because she wanted us outta the house, but she also didn't want us in the street. So in the early evenings, we'd go and play checkers or cards, run around in the basement, or play games on the grassy knoll outside.

Grandma's church was super-straight traditional Baptist. Couple hymns, stand up, sit down, stand up, sit down. Some might say it was boring and uptight, but not me in front of my grandma, unless I wanted to pick out my own switch. Her church wasn't shouty, jump-up-and-down-ish. That was more the style of my home field church in Atlanta. The Hillside Chapel and Truth Center had big personality. Starting with our preacher, the Reverend Dr. Barbara Louise King. She was a force of nature, and not just because she was six feet, six inches tall. She had this Jesus effect on people because she was so filled with the spirit. Larger than life, literally and figuratively. She had a custom Cadillac stretch limo built for herself, and nobody questioned that because she was six foot six. She needed a lot of legroom, I guess. She was a phenomenon, partly because, yes, she was a woman, still a rarity back then. It made our church feel special.

Hillside Chapel and Truth Center—it's called that because it was a "truth" church. Nondenominational, but they do study the Bible and try to take the truth from it. It's about the power of words and positive reinforcement. It's more open to everybody else's beliefs, as well. It's about trying to find the truth in whatever anyone's supernatural experience has been.

Hillside started as a small church but soon built a big church next door called "the Church in the Round." It matched the stature of our big ol' preacher (not literally—forgive me, Reverend Doctor). It basically had stadium seating. It also put on a big ol' show with big ol' special guest preachers from exotic faraway lands who put hands on people and they fainted. When I was seven, I watched my mom faint with my very own eyes. "How much do you believe in this?" I asked her after it happened. I was a mature seven; I must have already known Santa Claus was a lie. The visiting healer, from Trinidad, was reading into people's repressions and health issues without them telling her. She called my mom out on specific things she'd been struggling with and stressing over. "I never thought that I would like pass out like that," my mom said. "I believe." The healer then laid her hands on my chest and prayed on my lungs. I never forgot that. As I grew into my smoking years, I always wondered if that's what she might have been feeling back then. These clairvoyant kind of people, you know, their premonitions have nothing to do with time, necessarily. They can feel energies through parallel universes and the time belt itself. Thank you for coming to my TED Talk.

Other than the entertaining spectacle of the healers, I was a kid, so my reverend's half-hour-straight sermons, all that adult talk going over my head, was a total snoozefest. I always fell asleep, which annoyed my mom to no end. But the minister told her, "Let him sleep. He will absorb what he needs. Just leave him be." Don't get me wrong, I loved some of the stories—Abraham, Jonah and the Whale, David and Goliath—and the stories had pictures to back it up. It wasn't all that different from a Disney movie. I didn't want to bring shame on my family by falling asleep in front of everybody, so I got up and wandered around the church. I loved going up into the AV booth in the balcony to play with gadgets (or for a nap) or perusing the bookstore because it had gummy bears and delicious cookies.

Our church was a hot spot for the community's spirited entrepreneurs. The real Famous Amos used to come by to sell his wares. I met him a few times as a kid. He was a sweet, quiet old man, always smiling. And a skinny dude, which I found remarkable because he must have eaten thousands of cookies to get his recipe right. He brought bags of his amazing chocolate chip cookies, and they were moist and hot and the nuts in them were great (pause). Now they're kinda factory dusty, but the point is, his whole empire started in our community. Then he blew up for real, and it was awesome to see that kind of success. And let's not forget Gentleman Jim, which I thought was the greatest nickname ever, because it set a high bar for his intentions. He made designer dress vests, of course, and I was a big fan of a snappy vest, I cannot lie. When it was time for prom, I got my vest from Gentleman Jim.

Sometimes I took romantic strolls with my church honey. We met there, and she was one of my first loves. But she was my one and only church girlfriend, for sure. We were two kids just wandering around in the guts of a big building, finding little spots to hide out and flirt. It was very sweet. We were attached at the hip, very intrigued by each other. We really liked each other and we stuck with it for a while. It was another reason I didn't mind going to church all the time.

Black church shaped me, no question. Most important, it taught me how to be a man. I always enjoyed being around the elders of the neighborhood. You can't learn how to be a man without seeing one. All around me I had living breathing examples of men who looked like upright individuals, took responsibility, treated people with respect, and had good manners. Especially if they were married and they would just support their wives every Sunday by coming to church. That's what a man does. All the guys in the choir all seemed like very stand-up kind of guys to me, too, because, not to be chauvinistic, but it seemed like, you know, ladies did it better. So, for a guy to want to be in the choir, they must, like, A. be really good, or B. be just as dedicated as these powerhouse Black women I was used to growing up around.

With the church and God behind it, you really had to be a good person or else you were going to a bad place. It was all about being an upstanding member of the community and being active participants in your little microcosm. We were friends with everybody. My mom was quiet but very social. You could always hear her high-pitched laugh echoing in the gargantuan church hallways. She was always the last one to leave because she was talking to people. Every time we were ready to go home or head to the Beautiful for some okay breakfast, we'd spend a lot of time trying to find her. I remember being sent back multiple times by my dad with an exasperated "Go get your mama." My mom was always the last one in the car.

My family, we were always there, and we were big joiners—my dad was in the choir, my mom was an usher, her mom was an usher. So that meant we had to sing in the choir and, once we learned to play the piano, play for the church. The church is where my creative fire was first sparked. I got my singing chops from my dad and my mom.

They both can sing. But my dad was one of the soloists at the church forever.

My brother and I both joined the Atlanta Boy Choir, too, so I was used to performing as part of a group. In my mind I was a tenor, like Pavarotti, but since my voice hadn't dropped yet, I was more of a soprano, like Diana Ross. I got used to playing my tiny role and learned to step aside so others could get theirs. A friend at the time was a singer, and I was secretly jealous of all the attention he got. When he was late to a recital, I volunteered to step in his place for the big solo. The corn dog in me wanted to be a team player, to step in and save the day, even though I only knew about 10 percent of the words. When it came time for him to do his thing, which was now my thing, the lights shone so bright that I blindly opened my mouth, not knowing what would come out, when . . . my friend showed up to do his thing. Darn. That solo would have launched my singing career, I bet. This could have been a very different book. Sorry, music fans. Please enjoy reading about *Saturday Night Live* instead.

So anyway, I could sing, but I liked soul the best. Gospel was cool and all, because the best soul singers usually had a gospel background. I remember when the original *Dreamgirls* came to town, I was floored. I could not believe people could sing like that. Between *Dreamgirls* and *The Wiz*, good Lord. There's so much flavor in everything we do. When those of us who have the gifts to sing like Aretha or play like Quincy Jones or dance like Michael Jackson actually come together on a project and actually do it, it's gonna be dynamite. Let alone undiscovered actors on Broadway or in a musical like *Dreamgirls*, which was just filled with new talent. Unless you knew gospel, you didn't know Jennifer Holliday until *Dreamgirls*. That soundtrack put her on the map. What a voice.

But me, I wanted to skip that level and go straight to the funk. Singing in the choir was never really that interesting to me. Now, when acting was thrown into the mix, I really liked that. I did one of my first plays at the church. We did *The Wiz* one time, and I was too young to be one of the main parts. I didn't want to just be in the ensemble, so I asked Renee, the organist, "Can I be the dog?" So I played Toto and I was in every scene and I stole the darn show.

My memories of my childhood church are vivid and warm and loving, and I'm grateful it's part of my DNA. What it boiled down to was the fellowship. Atlanta was a migration kind of place: Black folks from all over the South came together here and latched onto a church. It's our anchor, our core, our community; it helped us get through the lower-middle-class existence. It really took a village, especially for my hardworking parents, who were doing their darndest to raise two kids.

As I got older, I drifted away from the religious lifestyle for a bunch of reasons. The first time I questioned it all was when I learned what a parable was, and whether the story was true or not, there was a lesson in it. It hit me suddenly, like, *Oh, this isn't necessarily a true story? It's just a blueprint for going through life? According to people who have done it so far?* That was eye-opening, and not necessarily in a bad way. Just in a self-evolving way.

Then it kind of hit me that in the Bible, they sum stuff up a little too easy. Like the Tower of Babel. I'm like, all right. So you're telling me that they built this tower and then by the time they were done, the people that were at the top were speaking different languages when they came back down and that's how language started all over the world? Bro, that's way too simple, and that's not true. I was having problems with it. I was also tired of having to interpret the decoding of the Bible, and all those stories. That's not enough? Now I have to go to China to understand the history of the Chinese language? Now I gotta go to Japan? It felt like an endless kind of an effort. So then I was like, well, instead of trying to learn about everything, why don't I just be open to whatever information comes my way? And not necessarily try to get a doctorate in the origin of Japanese culture and language? Maybe not be so obsessed and move on with life?

Then when I started high school, I decided I didn't need to go to church all the time. And not just 'cause I wanted to sleep in. I didn't feel the need to dissect every aspect of life's struggles through the Bible every single week. I could live life and be positive and go to work. I didn't necessarily have to look for clues in the Old Testament of how I should be approaching my day-to-day.

In my twenties, I decided organized religion was not for me. By this point, I was a legit celebrity, and actually showing up at church became a burden. Like signing autographs, which I always thought was weird at a place that I grew up in. These people had seen me every day of my life since I was five years old. They knew my name; they knew I took naps in the AV booth. Signing autographs made it seem like I was being treated and acting different, and I wanted to make sure that they knew I wasn't acting different.

I was up for the spirituality of it—if anyone wanted to talk about God or any of that stuff at any given moment, I was down. But any church I went to, it felt like the people who ran it always had an agenda with me, or wanted to use me to promote it. One lady needed me to help her bake sale. Where was Famous Amos when you needed him? The agendas just started flowing, and for me it was annoying because I thought we went there to just go to church. I didn't understand the extras.

Just getting out of there after a service became a headache, too, especially when I went with Kel. In our heyday, the two of us being seen together out in public brought great joy to many but also caused a logjam when getting out of the pew and through the exit door. People wanted to come talk to us, shake our hands, slap us on the back, and we obliged. Kel's very charming and very religious, even to this day.

In fact, Kel is even more religious than probably he's ever been. But we would go together because we were both raised like that. When we moved to LA after Nickelodeon moved the *All That* studio to Burbank, Kel and I were going to this church called West Angeles Church of God and Christ on Crenshaw in the historic Black community of West Adams every Sunday. It was a great church. "West A" boasted A-list parishioners like Denzel Washington, Angela Bassett, Magic Johnson, basically a who's who of Black Hollywood. It was a more traditional, celebratory Baptist vibe, the kind where the preacher shouted, "Hey, man, oh yeah!" with the organ during his sermon and when he was done preaching whatever lesson he chose. That was how he brought the energy back up. "Hey, man, oh yeah!" He built up to one of those moments where the music kicked in and everybody started dancing fast-paced, waving their hands, and fanning themselves. It was wild and inspiring. I really, really loved it because although we were in a big new city, it felt familiar. We went for a couple of years, but then it started to become a thing when people began trying to rope us into promoting their businesses. Church began to feel different, and the desire I once had soon faded.

My religious journey did a 180 for sure. Today, I don't go to church; organized religion isn't necessarily my thing anymore, knowing what I know now as an adult is the disclaimer. My spiritual journey is a much more personalized thing. Although it does say in the Bible that you should fellowship with others. At the same time, the Bible's not the only manuscript we have; we have a bunch of different books with guidelines in them. I'm supposed to just be calling myself a Baptist, but I agree with a lot of Islamic beliefs, Jewish beliefs, Buddhist beliefs. With so much going on in the world, I can't just be like, *If you don't believe in Jesus Christ, you're going to hell.* Like, that's crazy to me. What if you've never heard of the Jesus Christ story? Why should you be forced to go to hell because of that?

The common denominator of all of those books is the idea that "gathered together" is just love. In my opinion, be a good person and good things will happen. It's a much more generic approach for someone who's not necessarily out to do dirt anyway. I don't need to be wrangled or controlled or anything like that because I only wanna do positive in the first place.

I could never be an atheist—that seems so closed-minded to the rest of the world just because you think you know more than millions of people and their personal experiences. I don't have any regrets or pushbacks or moments of clarity where I'm like, *I can't believe they've been lying to me all this time!* It was me needing to process that mine wasn't the only religion. And it's not about who's right and who's wrong. It's more, what is that about and what does that mean? What does God mean to someone on the other side of the planet?

There are so many things I still love about religion and the church. I still say my prayer of protection. I love to pray. I pray every day. My prayer work is strong, and I believe in prayer work. I have a cadence of prayers that I say whenever I fly or before certain performances, when I feel like I need an extra blanket of courage. Or a need to set myself in a *don't trip* mindset. I still pray for others when I feel people need it. I have moments where I get into the Bible and try to read a chapter every now and again and start from the beginning. Not because I take it literally, like Jonah actually got swallowed by a whale; it's more metaphorical. But it always throws me off, because Genesis is, like, just a bunch of names. After the creation of the world, it's just names for thirty pages. It's chronicling all humanity from the beginning, but who knows if this is correct? It's all these shout-outs, but who knows if it's an accurate record?

My kids don't go to church, at least not regularly. They get a little taste of that life—their maternal grandma is very religious, so she takes them to a nondenominational church when we're in Florida during my hiatus from *SNL*. Her family is big into Jesus and prayer and laying hands and miracles and all that. But it's nowhere near the immersive religious experience I had. I think about my girls growing up without that church life ingrained in them, and I'm not sure if it's a good thing, a bad thing, or both.

I take full responsibility for their secular upbringing and will leave it up to them whether they want to go that route or not. The bottom line is that 99 percent of religion is seeking and giving love. That's the point. If they get anything out of the church, it's the kindness-to-others part of existing in society, manners, respect, trying to make the right decisions. They don't need to trip on Ecclesiastes 16 specifically. It's fine if they find a message in it and learn from it. Whether they're gonna wind up in heaven or hell, it's a nonissue in my house. More concerning right now is figuring out how I'm gonna explain the whole Santa Claus mystery one day!

FOUR

Being a Dad Sucked the Cool Right Out of Me

My daughters are my toughest crowd. I try to make them laugh, but I think they've heard enough from me, just from watching my shows. They think their mother is funnier anyway. They're not impressed. And I can brag all I want to them about meeting the most famous people in the world on a weekly basis, but this does not make me an especially groovy person to them, or anyone else, actually. Can I say "groovy"?

My kids are a bit rambunctious. Georgia has always been very inquisitive and funny. As soon as she was in a walker and free to move about the cabin, she'd find us. Whenever we would go into another room, she would come to the edge of the door and peek in, make eye contact and get the biggest smile on her face. I got really into reading my kids' zodiac and natal charts, so I know who she is—she's sweet and sensitive first of all. Certain music makes her cry. She's also very argumentative and a great debater, so she'd make a great attorney. Every family needs an in-house lawyer because they are very expensive, so I will be encouraging that route for free legal advice.

Anyway, my big girl is one of the biggest hams I've ever seen. She inherited the acting gene for sure. She loves when I read her a book like *Good Night New York City* and do all the characters' voices. Mr. Jenkins, the firefighters, the cabbie, the hot dog vendor. I shout, "Hot dogs here!" and she giggles. I think my performing vibe rubbed off on her. Now she likes to put on performances and do characters, too, almost like how I used to do them alone in my bedroom when my brother caught me laughing hysterically. I caught Georgia recording herself doing little monologues and posting them on YouTube. I was like, "Yo, you can't do that," but, using her scarily adept debate skills, she convinced me to compromise, and now she can make and post videos if supervised. Georgia's highly energized, adventurous, and athletic. She picks up every sport she tries super quickly, like riding a bike, Rollerblading, skateboarding, softball, basketball, football, all of it. She's also super smart and will have a lot of choices in life. I don't worry about Georgia.

It's not like I worry about Gianna, per se, but if you must know, she will scratch you. I'm just kidding, sort of. My baby girl is such a sweetheart, but she has a real devious side and sense of humor, too. She's just fearless and reckless, like a textbook youngest child. It's good to be fearless, but she does bump her head sometimes. You have to be careful with her. You want her to be adventurous but in a safe way. She went indoor skydiving the other day and loved it. She took right to it and did it the best out of everybody. She also loves witches and zombies and just being wicked basically. She's always teasing Georgia and playing pranks on us. Nothing makes her laugh harder than when she steals my seat right out from under me. She's a little rascal, God love her. Gianna's the one we have to watch, because she's a Leo. She's determined to get what she wants, and if she doesn't get it, it's the ultimate battle of wills. For example, if I put broccoli out and I didn't tell her first, it's a long conversation.

Most people don't know that while I film *SNL* in NYC, a lot of my personal time has been spent in Tampa, as a lower-middle-age, uncool dad. I was already a nerd, we all know this by now, but the day I became a dad, my geekiness elevated to a level that falls somewhere between hip hopster and hip replacements. I literally have a book of dad jokes on my coffee table, but I can never remember any of them. I guess your memory evaporates the less with-it you become. I didn't even feel this shift, but as soon as my babies arrived, I immediately started wearing black socks and shorts and being really corny at stores. I overask questions that have answers that are super obvious. One time I asked Georgia for a password, maybe for, like, the tenth time or I couldn't figure out how to log in to something, and she called me "bruh."

"I'm sorry, excuse me?" Did my ears deceive me?

"Bruh, you just do this." Then she tippity-tapped on my device at warp speed.

I stared at her in disbelief. Was I already the old man who shakes his hand before he pops peanuts into his mouth? Was I moments away from jingling change in my pocket? Geez. As far as technology goes, my girls are already running circles around me. I thought I had my act together, but nope. I gotta practice more to make sure I'm on top of it. I will make a conscious effort to text back more than "ok" to any future communication between my daughters and me. Today she calls me "bruh," but tomorrow it could be "Kenan." It's a slippery slope. I'm not one of those parents who'd be okay with my kids calling me by my first name. I don't know that there's a higher level of mockery than that.

"Kenan, would you put my Goldfish in a little baggie, please?"

"Can we get a hamster, Kenan?"

"Kenan, why do you sneeze so loud?"

I try to run a tight ship with the discipline, but I'm not quite as strict as my mom. I have to catch myself when I start sounding like my own parents. Especially when we're in the car and my girls are in the back seat. I have said the cliché, "I will turn this car around right now and we will go right back home. We will not be going to the zoo!" Everybody knows that's a lie. In the history of automobiles, has anyone ever actually turned the car around? Once the young ones catch on that you'll never actually turn the car around, you're toast.

I admit I'm a softie, some may say pushover, in certain ways. Whenever I pick my kids up from school, I always have to buy them a little trinket from the dollar store on the walk home. I don't spoil my kids with expensive things, because I'm pretty frugal, which I suppose in some circles would make me uncool. But I don't shop until I drop for myself, either. I'm not a sneakerhead. I wear one pair of shoes until they fall off my feet. Listen, I've got to send my children off to college. Kel recently looked down at my sneakers, made a stink face, and said, "Man, you still doing that?" Once they are unwearable, then I'll cave and get a new pair, but it's always the same shoe. I'm very fond of a low-top Nike Air Force 1. It's just a functional shoe. To be thrifty, I'm a color coordinator. I get fresh whites or black or gray or navy, so they go with a lot of different outfits and match my hoodies. I don't like high-tops, and I'm too old for, say, Converse Chuck Taylors, which have no ankle support at all. Plus, I have big hooves, so they make my feet look flappy.

It's okay, we can talk about my style—and the fact that I have none. Sure, I was brave enough to wear a neon pink suit to the Emmys, but then I avoided every comment section on the Internet for two weeks after so I wouldn't cry. Thing is, I like nice clothes, so I'll grab stuff here and there, but then I'll just hold on to them for forever, thinking that that's dope. (Does anyone say "dope" anymore? Where are we with "dope"?) But as far as, like, who's pushing things forward, it's certainly not me. When Jay-Z started wearing platinum and everybody started wearing platinum, then he went to gold and everybody started wearing gold, yeah, no, that wasn't me. I pretty much stick with one thing.

Obama has two daughters, like me, and he's someone I admire and idolize so much, except for that one time he wore dad jeans to throw out the first pitch at an All-Star Game. Am I on the precipice of dad jeans, too? Maybe it's inevitable. I did a thing with Old Navy recently and they hit me with a bunch of clothes, including actual pants and jeans. By golly, I'm wearing them. I didn't have any jeans before, but now I have five different shades of jeans—black, brown, gray, blue, white! So I've been showing up to work in pants instead of sweatpants, and I'm very proud of myself. It's a little jarring to wear pants that don't have elastic, and yet I feel like a more responsible adult. I've been combining my new pants with some flannel shirts and moccasins or loafers, and I've been getting such a positive response from the cast and crew. It's like, "Hey, man, you look like an adult!" And I say back, "Thank you, other adult!"

SOMETIMES I FEAR MY MUSIC TASTE HAS FROZEN IN TIME FROM THE '60s to the '80s. I may not listen to Lou Rawls on repeat like my old pal Steve Harvey yet, but it wouldn't be out of the question to catch me belting "Rubberband Man" or any other songs down that train, from the Philadelphia traveling band sound to Motown. I do listen to current music—Jay-Z, Childish Gambino, Two Door Cinema Club, and the Travis Scotts of the world. But my music library also technically includes Reba McEntire and Olivia Rodrigo. Is me listening to Olivia Rodrigo trying too hard to stay current? I don't play her on purpose, but if she happens to sneak up in the car, I'll belt out "Good 4 U" with the best of 'em.

My girls and I have such different taste in entertainment, and their reaction to what I watch on TV is a constant, humbling reminder that

I am no longer cool. One time I was watching a rerun of *Cheers*, and Georgia said the show reminded her of zombies walking around because it was so slow and boring. Then an actual commercial came on, and that was it for her. She totally checked out and bounced. Also, I've noticed that I turn the volume up to eleven lately, and my girls' little ears can't take it for too long. Maybe as I get older, my ears have too much hair in them, so I can't hear.

If I turn on football, they immediately leave the room. My girls' idea of quality programming is disappearing into the wild, weird world of TikTok and YouTube. Georgia watches people either explain or play video games like no tomorrow. I'm like, "Why don't you play the game instead of watching people play it?" It just doesn't sound appealing to me whatsoever, and that makes me feel old. What am I missing here?

Speaking of zombies, my face may still look as fresh as a baby's bottom—this Black don't crack—but if I'm honest, in many other areas of my life I'm aging somewhat ungracefully. My tootsies are looking a little wonky in open-toed shoes. I grunt when I get up but also when I sit down. There's also a lot of knee-cracking going upstairs. My baby girls love to climb up on top of me when I'm relaxing in a recliner and treat me like a human trampoline. I love it, but ouchie, especially when they fall asleep on me dead weight. I wouldn't dare move because it's so touching and adorable, but my limbs go numb, and I can't feel my extremities. That's scary for a fella heading toward half a century years old.

Daddy's tired. So very tired. I used to stay out all night; now I desperately need my eight hours of beauty sleep. I catch it where I can. I'm able to fall asleep just about anywhere: sitting up in a chair, standing up in front of the TV with my arms crossed, you name it. Then they'll poke me and say, "Are you sleeping?" and I'll say, "No, my angels, I'm just resting with my eyes closed," like all good dads do. Truth is, naps are an essential part of my life now. I go back to bed a lot in the daytime. Naps keep me on my toes and keep me celebrating the good things in life.

If all of what I just mentioned makes me uncool, so be it. There's nothing more creepy than trying to maintain coolness anyway. I think parents should be nerdier than their children, hands down. It maintains the right balance of power. I cannot wait for the day when I blurt out, "Money doesn't grow on trees!" or "They don't make 'em like they used to . . ." for the billionth time, and Georgia and Gianna roll their eyes behind my back and giggle and give each other a knowing look. As long as they don't call me "Kenan," everything's gonna be all right!

FIVE

How Watching "Programs" Can Become a Career

These days, my littlest one is always flipping around on YouTube Kids, and my big girl watches a lot of fake hacker videos, where she learns how to simulate breaking into a government computer system or digital network. It's really weird, and she's tricked me a few times into thinking I'm being spoofed with a brute-force attack or some shit like that. I guess everybody has their thing. As long as the FBI doesn't show up at our house with a search warrant and rip the stuffing out of our couches and leave all the cupboards open, it's harmless fun. Childhood passions can lead to lifelong careers. I mean, they don't have to. Just because your kid plays Taylor Swift on repeat until your ears bleed doesn't mean she's gonna sell out Madison Square Garden one day. I always wonder how my kids' random hobbies are going to shape their adult lives.

Georgia's interests are very vintage at the moment, from cosplaying Matthew Broderick in *War Games* to collecting and trading Pokémon cards. (They are back with a vengeance.) Georgia's into sports, and Gianna's into more girly things, like dolls, these days. She likes to strip them all naked and change their clothes a million times. She loves to wear her mom's heels and bags, and it's very sweet. I grew up with such a boyish childhood. We outnumbered my mom three to one. Now I'm outnumbered two to one.

All I know is, when I was my kids' age, I was manifesting my dreams without even really knowing what that meant. "Manifesting" wasn't even a thing back then. Seems like ever since the global pandemic, everybody's manifesting. Maybe that's because they all quit their jobs and have a lot of free time. I see that "Shut Up, I'm Manifesting" meme all over social media. As I type this sentence, there's a huge subculture of manifesting gurus on TikTok charging $79 a month to talk to you about your angel numbers at exactly 11:11 p.m. I might not have bought some crystals and done all that woo-woo stuff when I was six years old, but I'm telling you, I was manifesting like a little mofo.

When I was my girls' age, it was obvious that I was obsessed with television and one day would end up in television; I wanted to be in my television, literally. We were the family who had a giant wooden console in our family room, and when it blew out, we just set a smaller, shiny new TV right on top of the old console and left it right there for another decade. I really wanted to know how a TV worked. I'd look behind it, tap on it, but there were no people back there! At first, no one was willing to take the time to explain how broadcasting worked. Everybody was all, "Go sit in the corner and stop asking crazy questions!"

After watching *Bill & Ted's Excellent Adventure*, the zany Keanu Reeves film about time travel to other dimensions, I remember imagining myself climbing inside our big ol' box, flying through the wires, and traveling though time. I also loved a silly movie called *Stay Tuned*, in which a married couple of couch potatoes, played by John Ritter and Pam Dawber, were sucked into a hellish television set and had to survive a bunch of weird TV shows or their souls would be owned by Satan for eternity. Imagine *Black Mirror*, if it starred Jack Tripper and Mork's BFF-turned-lover Mindy. It was the craziest thing I'd ever seen. I was both intrigued and kinda scurred because there was a mean devil.

My generation predates cable TV. There was a short time when some of us had to get our butts up off our beanbags and crawl over to the console to change the channel. My love for television goes way back, stemming from watching "programs" with my grandma on her ol' black-and-white, which had a cable box that looked like a white keyboard. You'd move a cursor back and forth and up and down to find a channel. I'd get excited to get up early with her, then watch *The Price Is Right*. I loved the oddly melancholic theme song (listen to it again; it's kind of a bittersweet melody). I prayed the yodeler wouldn't fall off that cliff and dreamed of yelling, "One dollar!" and playing Plinko and Punch a Bunch and sinking a long putt for Hole in One. Bob Barker's tall, skinny microphone had a long-ass cord that draped dangerously across the stage, and I hoped nobody would trip over it after they won the Showcase Showdown and sprinted over to hug Barker Beauties Dian and Janice.

Back then, we only had three network channels—ABC, CBS, and NBC—and that was it. Whatever was on, that's what we were watching, whether *As the World Turns* or *The A-Team*. You had your testosterone-fueled whitey cop shows like *The Dukes of Hazzard* and *Starsky & Hutch*, and your saccharine-sweet sitcoms such as *Silver Spoons* and *Growing Pains*. I enjoyed the diversity of *Diff'rent Strokes* (is it just me or does that apostrophe seem a little racist in hindsight?) but was very confused when the housekeeper, Mrs. Garrett, disappeared then showed up at a boarding school on *The Facts of Life*, as if nothing happened and we wouldn't be mad she left Arnold behind. Of course, I watched all the Black shows my eyeballs could find, like *The Jeffersons, Amen, What's Happening!!*, and the unfortunately titled spin-off *What's Happening Now!!* (That's the best they could come up with? They figured they could slap a couple exclamation points on the end and call it a day.) I loved that show, though. What a cast of characters: Shirley and Raj and Dwayne. Rerun's suspenders alone should have won an Emmy. And how about that Dee? She had some serious attitude and the best deadpan one-liners ragging on Raj. They don't make 'em like Dee anymore.

Arnold and Willis on *Diff'rent Strokes* were Kerwin and me, 1,000 percent. That relationship cemented in my mind that I can be the younger, mischievous brother and my older brother will fix any hijinks I get into. Arnold and Willis represented my brother and me, but they also represented "the brothers," if you will. Anybody that was rocking an Afro and was of the same kind of mentality, like, *We out here for the people, we out here for the culture, the struggle continues*, was my jam. I liked *The Jeffersons*, but in real life, I didn't know any interracial married couples like Tom and Helen Willis. It didn't look familiar; it seemed forced. Like, Helen was hot—what did she see in Tom? But Rerun getting on Raj's nerves, and all *What's going on with your pocket of people on your street?*, was very much how it was for me and the people I knew.

I was a sucker for a fierce yet loveable Black woman on TV. I even watched the news—most kids didn't want to watch that—because there was an anchor on WSB-TV named Monica Kaufman Pearson who was Atlanta's hometown hero. She was really good at her job, and, you know, she could have been my mom. They looked similar, sounded similar. I just assumed all Black women were the same way. Monica Kaufman Pearson was our Oprah. So I maybe knew a little more about Atlanta serial killer Wayne Williams and Snow Jam, the blizzard of '82 that destroyed Atlanta, than most of my friends.

I didn't mind catching a little bit of Monica here and there, but most of all, I was a student of comedy as a kid. My earliest comedy memory was watching *The Tonight Show* with Johnny Carson. I saw adults wearing suits, smoking cigarettes, and talking to each other about things I didn't understand. It all went over my head. I was more interested in watching my dad, waiting to see when he laughed at a joke. I could tell when things really tickled him. I found that fascinating; what a joy it was to be tickled by things. Might be perverted, might not be. Sometimes it seemed like whatever he was laughing at was teetering on the edge of naughtiness, like little boys laughing in church.

I would watch *Saturday Night Live*, too, but I wasn't laughing at that, either. I was just watching from a distance, from down the hallway, over adult shoulders, not really getting the jokes. I saw Eddie Murphy dancing around and noticed how everyone was mesmerized by his charisma. As I got a little older, I got it. I idolized Eddie—he was genius in movies like *Coming to America*, *48 Hrs.*, and *Beverly Hills Cop*. Other than maybe Richard Pryor, there'd never been a Black leading man on the big screen quite like Eddie. He crossed—no, smashed—boundaries and genres and was raking in $3 million per movie, a fortune back then. Eddie was a rascal in *Beverly Hills Cop* but also an action hero. *48 Hrs.* wasn't really a comedy—it was more of a thriller, but still had so many hilarious one-liners and quotables. My favorite was the bar scene where he schools a bunch of honky cowboys: "I've never seen so many backwardsass country fucks in my life." We had *48 Hrs.* on VHS; we could just watch it. My brother and I had to sneak down to the basement because of the cursing, or we'd get in trouble, though.

Trading Places didn't have foul language, so we could watch that anywhere, anytime. I must've watched *Trading Places* five hundred times, even though it was kind of a Christmas comedy. If I didn't watch it on actual Christmas Day, it was like there was no Christmas that year. And when I say "Christmas," I really mean the entirety of December and January. The state of Georgia didn't really get snow like the Eastern corridor, so we watched *Trading Places* to get us into the holiday spirit. It gave me that cozy, festive feeling to see Valentine and Winthorpe III come together and triumph over the old, evil rich dudes. That movie really holds up and was way ahead of its time in calling out systemic financial inequality. But that's not why I loved it. It was Eddie's genius performance.

I had to sneak-watch his filthier cable TV stand-up specials, like *Raw* and *Delirious*, because Eddie was a lil' taboo in my house. I mean, the man was dressed in an extremely formfitting red leather suit, head to toe, and even I blushed. He tossed out "fuck" like candy in casual conversation. Maybe my mom secretly liked the red leather suit—we'll never know—but the cursing was a definite no-no. To give you an idea of how chaste my childhood was, I wasn't allowed to watch Prince's *Purple Rain* because a naked lady jumped into a body of water. When I eventually saw it, I thought, *That was it? That's what they were going on about?* My brother got his hands on VHS tapes of Eddie's comedy specials, and we watched them when our parents were out and about. They were always home at night, so we'd have to watch them at weird times on rare occasions. Didn't stop us from memorizing them verbatim and acting them full out for all our friends. We had Eddie down to a T—his cadence, the way he moved around the stage, the way he singsonged the legendary ice cream bit.

"You don't have no ice cream, you didn't get none, you didn't get none, you didn't get none, you didn't get none. Cuz you are on the welfare. And can't afford it. You can't afford it, you can't afford it.... And [your] father is a alcoholic.... Want a lick? Psych! You want some ice cream!... You cannot have some! You can't—"

CLUNK.

"You dropped your ice cream! You dropped your ice cream!"

Eventually, word got out to the adults that our Eddie impersonations were spot-on, and we got requests for impromptu performances.

Mom and Dad would have company over and call us into the living room. "Hey, do the little impression of the thing!" one of our aunties or uncles shouted out. Then we'd have to try to figure out which scene they wanted us to do 'cause they were horrible at describing it. "You know, do the thing! Like, the man and the other man!" Our performances were personalized, tailor-made for our audience. We'd feel out the room first and reduce sexy stuff and cuss words, if necessary.

I learned from Eddie what a rock star looked like onstage. He was crazy funny, but also a great storyteller—like Bill Cosby, but raunchier. In my mind, *they* were the two kings of comedy.

Eddie and Bill. The two men who shook me to my core and fed my comedic soul. But I really feel like my sense of humor was honed when I started paying attention to Bill Cosby. By this time, *Fat Albert* had come and gone already on Saturday mornings—I missed that by a few years—but I watched Bill on *Picture Pages* reruns every day. The high-pitched screech that his doodle pen, named Mortimer Ichabod Marker, made on his magic drawing board is burnt into my eardrums and memory forever. *Picture Pages* was the first time I identified Cosby's business brand: clean comedy. But the first time he made me laugh was reading his autobiography. He seemed very country-clubby to me, very established. Outside of music and rock stars, I didn't see a lot of representation of Black men in entertainment being financially stable.

The Cosby Show was life-changing to me for a few reasons. America saw the Huxtables, an affluent, whole Black family unit. We weren't seeing any single mothers or single dads, like on *Sanford and Son* or *What's Happening!!* We were seeing the Black family intact, which was very important because the media seldom portrayed us that way, and not placed in a white world, like *The Jeffersons*. I grew up in a segregated city, in my own Black bubble, so this made much more sense to me. The show also challenged traditional gender roles: Claire Huxtable was not a stay-at-home mom but a working attorney who practiced outside the house. Heathcliff was a doctor and was active in the rearing of the children, and not just as a disciplinarian. The kids were more scared of Claire than they were of Cliff!

The show was funny, but it wasn't preachy, even though it exposed us to a lot of things and opened our eyes. If you'd never seen Lena Horne, you got exposed to Lena Horne on *Cosby*. We were all in love with Rudy because there weren't a lot of young Black girls on TV—kind of just *Good Times* and *The Facts of Life* had them. And we were just like, *I'm in*, totally. If you'd never heard of HBCUs before, that's where you developed a sense of pride in America's historically Black colleges and universities. You woke up to the fact that there was another gold standard, other than Harvard and Yale.

The Cosby Show was the first time we saw Black excellence on display. Everybody was doing well, and all the kids were extremely well-behaved and motivated to excel. Being mediocre was not gonna cut it. It was not cool to be mediocre. One time the son, Theo, he wasn't a great student, and he brought home bad grades. And he tried to justify it by saying, "Dad, you're a doctor and mom's a lawyer and that's great, but maybe I wasn't cut out for that. Maybe I was just meant to be regular people. Maybe instead of getting on me, you should love me anyway because I'm your son." It was very eloquent and it was a beautiful TV moment and they even paused for studio applause. Cliff looked at Theo, paused dramatically, and said, "Theo . . . that's the dumbest thing I've ever heard in my life! No wonder you get Ds in everything! You are afraid to try because you are afraid your brain is going to explode and it's gonna ooze out of your ears. Now I'm telling you, you are going to try as hard as you can and you're going to do it because I *said* so. I am your father; I brought you in this world and I'll take you out!" It was so hilarious because it was the truth. And Black parents talk that way.

My parents approved of *Cosby*. Everybody did back then. His comedy was so squeaky clean, he was the first person where my mom said, "All right, you can watch him." *Great*, I thought, *then I'll watch everything he does!* I watched his comedy specials millions of times. I was floored. I couldn't believe someone could talk that long and that precisely. I was overly intrigued by the concept of the one-man show. It seemed like such a high-bar-setting kind of a performance. *Aha, this is what intelligent humor sounds like!* Because Richard cursed and Eddie cursed and Robert Townsend was different and the Wayans brothers were more silly and satirical. None of them had a two-hour special that I could watch a million times. Cosby's style spurred me to go beyond joking around with my friends and family. I got into the actual craft and creation of jokes.

Because Cosby talked for so long, and so brilliantly, people were so entertained. It felt like everybody could relate to every single thing he was saying. He was a dad and a successful guy, so everybody who fell into one of those two buckets was getting those jokes. But at the same time, I was only seven, and I didn't have any kids or a job yet, and I was getting it, too. I could quote every word of his specials. Like, the whole giving-birth bit where he has to get his wife to the hospital. "Don't do it in the $17,000 Ferrari, please."

What the what, he's got a Ferrari? I thought. That's the first time I connected the dots and saw a bigger picture of the entertainment world. When *Lifestyles of the Rich and Famous* popped up, I thought, *So this is what Cosby is living like. Interesting.* He must have everything that he could've ever dreamed of. I thought because his special was that good, he must be that good at life. The show was mimicking his life. So he's obviously got a nice family, a lot of kids, they don't have financial issues. *My God, their life must be amazing.* I put Cosby on a pedestal and left him there until I got a chance to do the *Fat Albert* movie myself years later. There was no question about Cosby being one of the greats. But then he chipped away at his own legacy, at first with certain comments about ghetto names, and eventually the whole temple crashed after multiple sexual abuse accusations. But I cannot deny the lifelong, lasting impression he made on me to do "clean comedy." It's who I am. That's my brand, too.

Maybe it's a cliché to say that representation matters, but clichés exist for a reason. In the '90s, I was going through puberty at the exact same time a ton of TV shows starring Black guys premiered. It was the golden age for Black male comics, and it had a profound effect on me at such an impressionable age. I had idols coming out of my ears. Martin Lawrence knocked down another door. He was the man; when *Martin* premiered, that's when the train really started. Jamie Foxx and the Wayans brothers with *In Living Color*, a sketch comedy show starring supremely talented Black dudes. Oh, let's not forget Jaleel White on *Family Matters*. Mark Curry in *Hangin' with Mr. Cooper*. Will Smith in *The Fresh Prince of Bel-Air*. Larenz Tate in *South Central*. The Black girl sitcoms were killing it, too, like *Thea*, *Moesha*, *Sister, Sister*, and *Living Single*. I gotta shout out the whole list because it was highly inspirational.

Everybody was making history and taking names. Let's not forget Arsenio Hall. No Black person had ever hosted a late-night show at that point. It was Carson and Letterman. He even predated Leno. Arsenio changed the game. He was such a breath of fresh air. He was legitimate—he scored exclusive interviews with Minister Louis Farrakhan, and also Magic Johnson to talk about his HIV+ diagnosis—but Arsenio was so fun. His guests were way looser than on Carson, who occasionally had a Black guest on but the rest of the time it was very whitewashed. It was hard for Black people to relate to what was going on. When Arsenio broke that barrier, you could tell by the format and the flavor of the show that they were letting him be himself. Oftentimes, as Black people in America, we code switch. Which means we will act differently in public, at school, at work, than we do at home. Because our natural way of being is usually frowned upon by white society. So we have to change the way we speak, change the way we walk, change the way we interact with people, and that can be exhausting. But it's what you have to do in order to get ahead.

Arsenio was not having the code switch. He could just be himself and not have to assimilate, and the rest of the world was coming in and enjoying it. We were all like, *Yes, there is hope for the future!* He was talking about things that we knew about and were interested in, and you could just let your hair down and relax. You didn't have to code switch anymore and could just watch TV.

Arsenio, by the way, was my first style influencer. Or was it Ricardo Tubbs from *Miami Vice*? Tough call. In the *Miami Vice* pilot, the very first episode, Tubbs, a cop, wore a silky gray double-breasted suit jacket and gold jewelry, and his trademark look single-handedly started a trend. We all know by now that I had a thing for vests, but I became a suit guy, too. Arsenio wore a spiffy new suit and tie every day of his talk show and, like, wut. I didn't even know that was possible! It was a fashion show every day. Arsenio was mint condition night after night, never a hair outta place, he even looked like he smelled good, like maybe he was exuding the cashmere musk of Michael Jordan cologne. I didn't know you could wear suits somewhere else other than church and still be fly. And he was friends with everybody, from Eddie Murphy to Michael Jackson.

Arsenio was *cool* comedy.

He made white people cool, too. Like when Bill Clinton played the saxophone with Arsenio's band, or he let Vanilla Ice speak in defense of white rappers. How about when Jim Carrey came on and pretended to be drunk? Once I was introduced to Jim Carrey, I felt like he was one of the most dynamic performers I'd ever seen, and he didn't disappoint from that moment on. This guy was emoting every single possible fraction of a second that he could. It's almost like his body expressed words more than his mouth. His starring role in *The Cable Guy* is probably the greatest comedic performance on film. He was and is a genius.

There came a point when I was like, *Okay, I've got the Black comedy genre down pat*, and realized to be a true scholar on the subject, I had to study the white side of it, too. My philosophy became, *Anything comedy, just bring it my way.* Jim Carrey led me to other physical comedians like the late, great *SNL* star Chris Farley. He was just as funny as anybody else, and he made really smart references and did really smart voice character work. His sense of humor was actually very sophisticated. It wasn't just about falling down, but that schtick was brilliant, too. He was the first comedian I saw who was a freight train, just throwing out wild shenanigans. Cosby was a guy in a chair with his legs crossed—your dad talking to you. Farley was running through literal walls, but also just tossing out gems of quick hits that you maybe didn't notice because he was smashing through a table. Farley just blew my mind.

I started looking back at classic white shows like *Taxi* (brilliant ensemble comedy) and *Maude* (political comedy) and *Newhart* (straight man/deadpan comedy). White stand-up comedy vs. Black stand-up back then was interesting. It felt like white comedians talked about the full gambit of things, whereas Black stand-ups did comparison comedy of white and Black culture. Like, "If white people have a picnic, they do it like this. If Black people have a picnic . . ." It really worked because the next comparison was going to get a reaction; since everybody was ahead of the joke and would be cheering by the time you got to the punch line.

The way John Mayer practiced his guitar and orgasm faces for ten thousand hours, I got my ten thousand hours of clowning cred by watching hours and hours of funny TV shows. But imagine if John

Mayer hadn't had access to a guitar. Starting at a very young age, I desperately wanted to channel my obsession with television into something tangible. But I lived in Atlanta, and Hollywood seemed like a far-off land of make-believe. It didn't seem possible at all.

Call it fate, kismet, dumb luck . . . at the exact same time I was manifesting my face off, Atlanta's first local cable station, SuperStation TBS, was cracking. TBS was a big deal, between running the Braves baseball games and the reruns I was watching incessantly. TBS popped up and killed the game as far as, like, the marathon is concerned. They were just like, *This is what we do, baby. This is your favorite? Here it is again for another hour. Oh, you like that hour? Here's three more hours!* I remember driving past the TBS studio downtown for the first time ever, seeing the giant satellites, and putting two and two together. *Holy shit,* my little brain thought but I didn't say out loud because my mom was driving, and I didn't want to get a swat from the front seat. "They're doing television right there?" I asked. "That's how they broadcast a signal? That's the place where they do it?"

"You'll learn about it someday," she said with a little smile.

My mom may have been strict, but she was pure love and her kids' biggest champion. As a parent, it's important to not only recognize your children's passions, but nurture them, because you never know where it will lead. That's what my mom did for me, bless her heart. Right before my tenth birthday, my mom, working full-time as a nurse, picked up a second job as a receptionist at the Alliance Theatre in downtown Atlanta, just so I could take acting classes there.

I owe her everything.

SIX

Your Daddy Was a Child Star
(and He Made It Out Alive)

Given my past as a child star, people always ask me, "Would you want your girls to follow in your footsteps?" Well, that's a tricky question. I would encourage them to pursue anything they're passionate about, even if it was becoming a singing ventriloquist. I mean, kids nowadays can rake in millions of dollars for being an Instagram influencer or an ASMR artist, putting people to sleep with crinkling plastic bags. You couldn't come close to making that kind of money during the time I grew up, unless you were Emmanuel Lewis, a drug dealer, or a professional tennis player. But I'd *definitely* keep a close eye because it's a slippery slope. My brain should be removed and studied by scientists because I'm one of the rare child actors who didn't end up dazed and panty-less on the cover of *Us Weekly*, or worse, on Dr. Drew's speed dial. I'm gonna try to explain how I escaped unscathed the best I can.

Girls, your daddy went the Emmanuel Lewis route. I got into the entertainment business at the tender age of five after I garnered rave reviews as the Gingerbread Man in an otherwise panned kindergarten Christmas production. Performing was my destiny, according to my mom. I guess because I was the second child, I felt alone and always had imaginary friends that I engaged in animated conversations, maybe about pooping my diaper, Lady Di's stunning wedding dress, or whatever else was going on back in the early '80s. One time when I was about seven, my brother walked past my room and my door was shut, but he could hear all these voices hysterically laughing and carrying on. He went to tattle to my mom.

"Mama, you said I couldn't have company, but Kenan's got company."

"No, he doesn't."

"Yes, he does. I heard him. I put my ear to the door and everything."

"Go to your room."

Kerwin slinked back to his room, but he wasn't satisfied. He snuck back to my room, turned the doorknob really quietly, peeked inside, and saw that I had toys and action figures all over the room and was doing different voices for every single one of them. I completely fooled my big brother and was just having a good time.

From a young age, I was "self-contained and self-entertained," my mom always said.

I channeled my pretend acting into actual performances in school productions first, then church plays. Even as a young performer, I never let anyone help me run my lines. I wanted to do my own interpretation; plus, it's also how I taught myself to read. At church, I sang and danced in an ensemble piece called *Kids Under Construction*, then when I was about eight, I landed the role of Toto in *The Wiz*. I wore the same brown onesie from my lauded Gingerbread Man performance, just added a tail. I didn't have any lines as Toto, not one word, but I stole the show, according to people who were there. I don't toot my own horn, because if I ever dared, I'd get a "disappointed" look from my mom that translated to *Don't even*. The Thompsons weren't raised as braggarts.

From early on, I was always getting mom love. Not just from my own. Basically, any mom anywhere, but especially in an audience. Even in the dark from the stage, I could see their little smiles and enchanted head tilts that meant, *Awww*. I got a strong cuteness factor going for the moms. One lady in the choir—Miss Sadie Bell, we called her—was the first person to put my photo on the church's "Wall of Fame," before I was anyone or anything. Our church organist introduced me to legendary character actor Freddie Hendricks, who founded the Freddie Hendricks Youth Ensemble of Atlanta. My brother, Kerwin, and I joined his theater as musicians at first. And yet another of my mom's friends, charmed by my charisma, told her, "You really need to do something with that little boy. He's extremely gifted."

"With what dollars?" my mom said. Times were tight. My parents had a mortgage and car payments, and Kerwin and I were begging for Green Machine Big Wheels. (I also once asked my mom to buy me a Stradivarius trumpet, which cost $1,000, and she scraped together the funds. It's still at my mom's house today collecting dust.) Wouldn't you know it, my mom's friend paid for my first acting classes, $90 for six weeks on Saturday mornings at the Alliance Theatre at the Woodruff Arts Center. It really does take a village. I kept asking my mom to take more classes, so she paid for the next sessions, then arranged a barter agreement with the school. She volunteered to write the credit card charges on the slip of paper. This was way before you could just tap your card on a machine like a wizard; somebody had to do it manually. One summer the school offered a three-week-long, all-day intensive workshop. To enroll me in that, too, my mom officially got a second job at the theater walking twenty-five kids across the street to get lunch at the mall every day. She did all of this while working nights full-time as a nurse. Sometimes, for convenience's sake, she'd take my brother and me with her to the hospital at ten p.m., put us in the bunk beds in the call room, and do her shift. She couldn't always be a million places at once.

My parents made a lot of sacrifices for my acting career, like enrolling me in an expensive private middle school that had an excellent theater department, so I could balance academics with my acting and stop commuting downtown alone. They knew, and I knew, at a very early age that I was super serious about honing my craft. When I was only eight years old, I won an award for my role as Mr. White Cat in a local production of *Hansel and Gretel* at the Fairburn community theater. I never heard of no Mr. White Cat, but no matter. This was my first real theater job; I mean, there were curtains and stadium-style audience seats. We performed to a sea of pitch-black, but I could hear reactions and laughter out of the shadows. It was like a drug. This was it. What I knew I wanted and needed in my life. And something I seemed to be able to do well.

Thank heavens for Mr. White Cat. That little scamp changed the trajectory of my life. I was like, *Forget about it, I'm an actor now.* I was inching my way toward whatever my involvement in the entertainment biz was gonna be. I didn't know what it was yet, but I felt I was getting closer. I knew comedy was my calling card. But I still had no idea how to get where I was going. I remember driving by the SuperStation TBS studio in Atlanta knowing deep in my bones that I belonged in there and hoping Steve Urkel from *Family Matters* was in the building. I still didn't know how TVs worked.

I was ready to take my career to the next level, so my mom forked out more money for a "Marketing Your Child"–type class at the Alliance Theatre school. I had to get professional headshots and find representation. Mom drove me all the way over to JCPenney on the other side of the airport to buy me a new sweater for my headshots; I didn't get a haircut, though. I thought my little Afro was adorable. Maybe that was our mistake. Or the fact that the photographer took two shots and proclaimed, "We're good. I think we got it."

We met with one Black agent in downtown Atlanta, and he took one look at my headshot and turned his nose up. My mom was offended.

I eventually found an agent to represent me, and he sent us on lots and lots of auditions. I remember my very first one at a Turner studio and seeing all of the satellites in the parking lot and getting a happy pit in my stomach. I asked for this without knowing it was a possibility at all. But then I walked into the room, this world of adults, and I felt like such an impostor. *What am I doing here?* I thought, panicking. *I don't even know how any of this works.*

I was a little naïve, sure. But not a rube. And this particular agent never, ever, ever helped me find a job. Never, never, never. So I switched to another agency, which sent me to auditions at a little cottage house with a white picket fence down a hill in a cul-de-sac in Buckhead. It was a little ragtag, but they cast commercials and worked really hard for me. It took a minute for me to land anything. Everybody knew I was good—one of the best child actors around—but I wasn't the "look" for leading roles. I was a chubby little Black boy. I wasn't a skinny blond kid with blue eyes. Even in school plays, that had been a factor. I thought maybe if I was in better shape, I might be more versatile. And that's why the quarterback was getting the leads. That stuff was in the back of my mind, but sacrificing who I was for the sake of a six-pack was not my agenda at that time. My agenda was having fun. I didn't have a shortage of that, so I didn't feel like I needed to cut anything out of my lifestyle. I still had girlfriends, and they saw me as cute. So I didn't see being on the rounder side of things as being too big a hindrance.

Still, I got an early schooling on rejection, an ingrained molecule in an actor's DNA. Luckily, I was young enough to not know I should dwell on it. At the time, I was still playing football and lettering in band (yes, band nerds got letters, too; I loved wearing my jacket) and doing all this other stuff, so it wasn't the be-all and end-all. My mom was proud that I never whined. "You don't have to do this," she said. "This is for fun. So if you don't wanna come back anymore, we don't have to." My vibe was always, *Let's see where it goes.* I wasn't ready to give up. I knew persistence mattered because once you're on their radar, you give casting agents a better idea of what you'd be good for, and therefore have a better chance of actually booking something.

I booked my first commercial for Lee's Famous Country Recipe Chicken, a chicken chain based in Nashville. The shoot was in Tennessee, and my dad came with me because my mom had to work. At least that's what they told me. I was blissfully unaware that my parents were not doing well and on the verge of divorce.

Shooting for Lee's Famous was definitely a learning experience. I had auditioned with one guy, but when I showed up on film day there was a different guy playing the part. I didn't really understand that they can just change things willy-nilly. Now I had to get to know another adult male stranger person. I didn't love that, but the guy was nice. He had a little skipper hat on. It was a fun commercial shoot because I got to eat free chicken. But the same time, I had an inkling the commercial was racist. Those kind of commercials back then always seem that way, even if they're not trying to be. In the commercial, I was supposed to be fishing with my granddad. My line was, "Grandpa, the fish ain't biting today." And he hands me a piece of chicken, and I eat it and say, "But I like this kind of biting." The director kept telling me, "Take a bigger bite, bite the chicken!" How much chicken could my little mouth hold? It was like, *Hey, man, you don't have to exploit the fact that Black people like chicken like that.* But then I looked over at Skipper and he was taking gargantuan bites of his chicken leg and not batting an eye. If he was doing it, I guessed it was all right for me.

After we were done, they paid me $800, and I was like, *What else you need me to eat? Where's the collard greens? I'll eat those, too.* I understood why the skipper shrugged it off, even if we both knew.

Booking commercials was a slow start, but once I booked one, it was like dominoes falling. I later filmed commercials for Sonic and played the role of "kid helping pull tire out of a car" for Publix supermarkets. I was pretty happy with my résumé so far. I didn't have bigger dreams at this point other than getting into the local commercial scene, so I thought I'd already made it. When I was in middle school, I booked a gig as a kid correspondent for these ABC News specials about two new exhibitions at Zoo Atlanta. As if the gig could get any dreamier, we shot at night, after hours, so I got to zip around Zoo Atlanta in a golf cart through a virtually human-less zoo. Just myself, the crew, and the giraffes, chillin'. Being an essential part of this supercool, vacation-like "work" environment made a lasting impression. It made me feel like a part of something greater. Performing was never about getting attention. It was about being an excitable bumblebee, who loved buzzing around the hive where everything was happening.

Another ABC special filmed in Grand Junction, Colorado, but neither of my parents could take me. My mom prayed long and hard about it and ended up sending me alone, deep within the Rocky Mountains, with a crusty old paleontologist and a TV crew of strangers. She figured the blessings of God were looking over me; she had to trust that it was going to be okay. We worked every day for a week, and on the final day, the director was running late and had to get permission from a guardian to let me continue. "Please, Mommy," I begged on the phone. "Please let me stay and finish." My mom let me do my job. The show won an Emmy.

That experience led to my first national TV show, reviewing movies for TBS's *Real News for Kids*. Shout-out to Monica Kaufman again for my lifelong interest in current events!

The Alliance Theatre school recommended me for the job; I never even had to audition! All I had to do was go see movies like *Aladdin* and *Angels in the Outfield* for free and judge them on a popcorn scale. The very first review I did was *The Mighty Ducks*—basically *The Bad News Bears* on ice. I didn't even know Atlanta had a hockey rink. I didn't understand ice being in the South. It's hot down there.

Anyway, I got to interview the cast at an old, dark hockey rink tucked away somewhere downtown. First of all, it was awkward; they kind of put on airs. Their attitude was, *We're movie stars; who are you, kid?* Second, I stared at Brandon Adams, the one Black kid in the movie, with doe-eyed wonder, like he was an endangered species behind glass at the zoo. I'd never seen a Black person play hockey; plus, he was in Michael Jackson's "Smooth Criminal" video. Like, *What is happening here?* JD Daniels was with Brandon and he was in *CB4*, which was super cool to me because he played Phil Hartman's son who loved gangsta rap. Huge fan of Phil!

I felt like such a nerd. I wanted to be as cool as Brandon—actually, all of these young actors. I asked my dumb little questions, and they couldn't have cared less about giving me a good answer. They were nice, but they were not trying to be friends with me. I was envious but highly inspired. I wanted to do this. I would stop at nothing to do this.

So, instead of making me insecure, meeting the cast kicked my butt into gear. A year later, on tax day, April 15 (my mom never forgot that), I, Kenan Stacy Thompson, auditioned for *D2*, the sequel to *The Mighty Ducks*. Separately from my review, my agent had submitted me for the sequel. With zero hockey or ice-skating experience whatsoever, it was as long a shot as running for US Congress. Through some stroke of luck, the casting director, without seeing my review, liked my headshot and asked me to send a self-tape. And then another. And one more. In a time before digital cameras, we were practically running out of money for all these tapes. Finally, they asked me to come to LA for the final audition.

It was a whirlwind couple days of being in a strange place. I'd never been west of Texas, but now I was thrust into the biggest version of the industry I had seen to that point. I was auditioning against real kid actors, like Baha Jackson, who played little Ice Cube in *Boyz N the Hood*. That was the biggest Black movie of my time as far as I was concerned. It was my *The Color Purple*. I felt like a country bumpkin coming to see my big-city cousins. I was overwhelmed, but I killed it and got my first movie role. And, PS, Baha wasn't so friendly that I felt bad about beating him. He was a little cocky—not toward me, he just had that air of confidence I longed to have. He thought he had it in the bag.

When I found out I got the part of Russ Tyler, my mom and I were literally jumping up and down. We could not believe it. My mind was blown, and I couldn't wait to go to California again. I was so pumped. But I was also worried: I had listed "roller-skating" as one of my skills on my résumé. Roller-skating was definitely not a skill I possessed. I couldn't roller-skate, blade, or derby for nothing, and I had the baseball-sized knots in my elbow to prove it.

By Mother's Day, I was in LA on the set. For the rest of the summer, my mom and I stayed at the Oakwoods and became absolutely enamored with Hollywood. Motorcycle cops like on *CHiPs*! Warm weather! Mexican food! In LA, we could walk around the corner and have the biggest burrito I'd ever seen in my life. And this was how much . . . $2.75?!

I started mandated hockey camp on May 10, my fifteenth birthday, which sounds so fun, but man, I'd lied about even being able to roller-skate. I was awful; I fell so many times on the cold, hard-ass ice. I was doing splits. I don't do splits. After the first day, my body was so bruised and battered, I told my mom I didn't want to be an actor anymore if I had to do this. I wanted to throw my swollen, blistered feet into the Pacific Ocean. I pouted. "Adult actors cheat! How come they get stuntmen, but we have to skate *and* play hockey at the same time?" My mom didn't pressure me, but she didn't want to let me quit, either, just because I wasn't having fun.

I was also dealing with being the new kid on the block and trying to fit in. That's hard to do when you look like a buffoon. The vets from the original had a certain swagger about going to work every day and balancing their school-work life. They were everything I wanted to be.

During my very first scene, I had to ride down a mad hill by UCLA on Sunset Boulevard on Rollerblades up to a fence opening and stop like a boss where the other kids were playing hockey. I didn't fall, but I was definitely putting on an attitude of being the tough kid from South Central and let that be my armor. I'm not even from South Central, not even close. My name, Kenan, means "stoic," but nobody needed to know that my nickname as a kid was "Pooh" because I had a Pooh Bear toy until I was fifteen.

Once the rest of the cast all saw I had athletic ability, everything else opened up. It was very tribal. We started skating together, and we bonded. There was the captain, and everybody else. It was obvious the ones who were there and took it very seriously and wanted an entire life as an actor. Then it was obvious the ones who were there for looks and then the ones who were there randomly. Between those three dynamics I could tell where I wanted to be. I wanted to be the serious actor. I wanted to be around this constantly. I thought it was the coolest thing, and I'd never felt more at ease. Yes, there was stress around performance time, but I felt very at home performing.

We had so much fun, but it was work. It was hockey, hockey, hockey, then we'd go home, try to do some homework, and pass out. The new kids all hung out with each other. We would all play Rollerblade hockey on some tennis courts, but honestly, we were pooped. My best friend on the movie was Ty O'Neal; he played the cowboy. When my mom would have to leave town, his dad would watch me. They were very sweet people. Even though Ty's dad, Bob, would pull on our big toes to get us out of bed. It hurt!

The fictional team was a Benetton poster—you had, amongst others, your heartthrob (Joshua Jackson), a ginger, a girl, and me, the chubby, funny Black kid. My role, Russ Tyler, was pivotal because it was known that I was going to be the semi-hero of the movie. I also had my own signature move, the infamous knuckle puck, which helped me stand out from an ensemble cast of awesome young actors and cemented my status in pop culture history and the sport of hockey. It was like being the Wild Thing in *Major League* or All the Way Mae in *A League of Their Own*. Maybe I wasn't the star of the movie, but, once again, I had those scene-stealing moments that everybody would remember forever.

D2 was that much of a pivotal part of my existence and so many other people's, especially in the hockey world. Any current NHL players that came of age during that time definitely grew up on that movie. It's a staple. In hockey towns, entire high schools would watch *The Mighty Ducks* in their auditoriums. To this day, I am able to go to hockey games with the extra-special VIP treatment at any given moment. If anybody wants to let me drop the first puck, or put some skates on, I'll show you how good I am. For a time, when we used to say our good nights on *SNL* at Christmastime, we'd go skate around under the tree at Rockefeller Center. Everybody would be blown away because I'd be zipping around the ice.

It was while filming *D2* that I auditioned for *All That*.

AS I MENTIONED, I WAS KIND OF COCKY, COMING OFF LIKE I WAS *ALL that* because I was on a movie set. But I was doing cartwheels in my mind because all I'd ever wanted was to be on TV. And I made it a reality.

When my mom and I headed down to Orlando from Atlanta, the first few days weren't exactly fun. At this point, my parents had split up, and my Spidey sense could tell this was all really rough on a new single mom, especially being away from her other son. But we got into the groove as best we could. It was good, good times in the beginning, so innocent. It was a "the world is our oyster" kind of mentality almost every day. At the first table read, our parts were already set and assigned. I was told, "You're doing a superhero who's lactose intolerant." That's all they gave me for Superdude, and boy, I ran with it. I found a voice I liked for him, and in rehearsal, I practiced posing with my arms akimbo, looking up to the light. I wasn't thrilled about jumping into tights to fight the Milkman, but I was willing to do whatever it took to crush my very first sketch. Superdude was the first character that I ever owned, so I embraced the humiliation. I escaped into the character so I wouldn't think about my thighs rubbing together or who'd be looking at the size of my wiener.

I'll never forget sitting backstage before the first taping, in the fall of 1992. I was only fourteen years old and had no idea I was about to make my wildest dreams come true. Fifty lucky theme park enthusiasts were sitting in bleachers, in front of a set made to look like backstage. Through a little Hollywood—well, actually, Orlando—magic, a PVC tube was rigged to my hat to make it look like I was sweating buckets. No one knew I didn't need the contraption. My nerves were working themselves into a light sweat. Some of the other cast members stopped by and tried to calm me down. "Think of all the people watching at home. Your friends, family, girls!" Kel reminded me. *Thanks, buddy.* The light sweat turned into a full-on waterfall. "All your classmates, teachers, doctors!" Alisa chimed in, almost slipping on the puddle now forming at my feet. It was so bad they could have used a squeegee on my face.

By the next episode, my eccrine glands relaxed, and I didn't need a team of towel boys to mop my brow. And I started to really enjoy myself. I soon developed my favorite sketches: "Mavis & Clavis" with Kel, about two old guys with a passion for song and dance; Dullmont Junior High's Principal Pimpell, who only wanted to talk about his pulsating pimple; the crazy lunch lady Miss Piddlin, who had anger management issues and was obsessed with peas, singing "Give Peas a Chance" (Miss Piddlin was one of the first female characters I ever did and wouldn't be the last); Lester Oaks, a character I'd revise in the "Good Burger" bit (originally, he was a hangry construction worker who used "construction" as a verb and could eat forty hamburger patties on one bun); and, of course, Pierre Escargot, likely my most iconic and beloved *All That* character, a bumbling, loveable dude who sat in a bathtub in a raincoat and scuba flippers, throwing out fake French terms the way any kid who didn't speak French would. Pierre Escargot was originally supposed to be a Spanish dude named Paco Delicious. It was borderline problematic racism-wise, so our writers went with French. They didn't want to wade into any discriminatory issues and get canceled before canceling was even a thing.

Pierre didn't teach children real French—he actually mocked the language and made up fake words. I take full responsibility for that; my bad. I could have spoken Spanish because I had taken it in school. I mean, everybody's got the "*Dónde está el baño?*" down. The basics. But French is super hard. It was already hard enough sitting in a bathtub in an awkward position on Styrofoam. My legs kept falling asleep. At first, the writers were sending me tapes with a French tutor, as if I were supposed to learn French from scratch. I put my flippered foot down. There was no way. My mom already made me do all my real homework like a nerd. Gibberish it was!

Did I know what I was doing? Hell no. I could easily create a coherent monologue off the cuff, but I was just beginning to hone my own comedy voice. One rule I figured out early on was, you can't be too big, too soon. On the flip side, being energetic and giving of yourself is always well received. Sometimes words weren't enough to heighten the comedy and some sort of physical antic could elevate an emotion: anger, fear, frustration. I taught myself how to make the exact face, almost like the pain scale emojis at the doctor's office. You could say this was the origin of the "Kenan Reacts" phenomenon. Years later on *SNL*, it was said that if a writer wanted a guaranteed laugh in a spot, they'd write in the script "Kenan Reacts."

I really didn't learn my own comedy voice on-screen until years and years later. My goal at that point was finding characters on their feet, putting voices to faces, and letting the words guide me. Once I saw a costume, that really locked my voice in. I looked at myself in the mirror, and it was like, *Oh, this guy sounds like this to me.*

The one voice I had down from the start during *All That* was my Cosby impersonation, which probably got me the job in the first place. So the writers crafted a parody of *The Wizard of Oz* called "The Wizard of Cos" for me. It took all day to shoot. Poor Josh was Mr. Mc-Toad, which isn't even a character in *The Wizard of Oz*. Josh had to wear this full prosthetic bald head with frog lips, and he was in it for fifteen hours. There were no labor laws for child actors in Florida at the time, so the shoot went on and on until we were done. I felt bad because I was dressed as Bill Cosby, in a cozy sweater and slacks, just chilling.

I was a famous TV star now, but that also didn't mean I could misbehave. My mom couldn't be with me all the time, and gave me three rules I had to follow, or I'd be shipped back to Atlanta, stat. Number one: academics came first, always. I had to do my homework regardless of everything else and whatever everyone else was doing or not doing. Number two was respect—for her, for myself, and the people I worked with. I could never, ever disrespect the crew. Oh, and obey Ms. Rita

Mitchell, Kel's mom, without question. She didn't play, either! Three, language. I remember one time we were in the middle of filming a scene when all of a sudden, my mom burst through the studio door like the Kool-Aid man. From all the way outside, she thought she heard me deliver a line with an inappropriate word in it. "Didn't I tell you no cursing? Nope, nope, nope, nope!" she scolded. When she realized that the *Do Not Enter* light was on, she apologized, because people apologized back in my day; there was no such thing as "doubling down." She owned it. It was so funny and so embarrassing.

She had no shame about it. In fact, she disciplined other people's kids, too. Sometimes there'd be an hour or two when another parent needed to leave for a couple hours and would sign guardianship over to my mom. A couple of my cast members had the audacity and, frankly, the bravery, to say to her, "Well, you're not my mama, and I'm gonna do what I want." And my mom would say, "No, you're not. I'm your mother for these two hours and you're gonna do as I say." To this day, they all call my mom "Mama Ann." She loves that.

I got the best training on *All That*. It was hands-on, learn-as-you-go trial by fire, and as time went on, I figured out how to do this sketch comedy thing. We all did. We would have a table read, then go rehearse. Then we'd ad-lib at rehearsal. We started noticing our ad-libs were making it into the script, and that became the game. The bulk of performing eventually landed on the shoulders of the oldest kids—myself, Kel, Lori Beth, and Josh. We called ourselves the Four Horsemen. The male cast members—Josh, Kel, and I—were all strong performers and could hop in and out of characters. The girls all had their strong performances, too. We looked up to Lori Beth so much, even though she was as green as the rest of us. At seventeen and the oldest cast member, she had that maturity glow. None of us was necessarily interested in the writers' room, except for Lori Beth. She hung out with the writers because we were too immature for her. It's not like we were talking about video games, girls, and farts all the time, but I imagine three teenage guys weren't all that intellectually stimulating.

Lori Beth knew good comedy and smart humor. With her signature sketch, Lori implemented perfect comedic timing. When she'd lose her mind and go off, I'd laugh so hard. Her performance of the sketch reminded me of *Three Amigos!*; she was in her zone and hit it out of the park every single time. When I'd look at Lori Beth in action, she'd make me think: *We're doing real comedy here.*

OUR RAPIDLY GROWING AUDIENCE AGREED. NICKELODEON BEGAN investing money into more advertising for *All That*, and included us in the two-hour programming block branded as "SNICK" (Saturday Night Nickelodeon) and aimed at older teen audiences. The fledgling network did not have super-deep pockets—we were lucky to be able to order in Wendy's once in a while (I loved making myself a loaded baked potato with all the fixin's)—so it was a big deal that they were putting so much investment into promoting us. By our third season, the show moved to Los Angeles to film, and Kel's and my partnership was so popular, they gave us our own spin-off, *Kenan & Kel*. We both turned eighteen around then, and we were officially on our own in the lion's den known as Hollywood. It was just us feeling like real grown-ups. I even got my own apartment, my very first, in Beverly Hills, 90210, right next to the Beverly Center. My apartment wasn't as fancy as it sounds, nowhere near Aaron Spelling's sprawling estate with the bowling alley in the basement. But it was my place.

It was a ginormous time for Kel and me, in each of our respective careers. We were workhorses, grinding all day and night on two shows (and sometimes burning the candle at both ends). *Kenan & Kel* was a sitcom, a totally different format than a sketch comedy show, so we were in 98 percent of the scenes. Executing a scripted sitcom properly commanded a different kind of skill set, one that didn't rely on the use of wigs and costumes but rather the development of characters and narrative plots and story arcs. As best friends Kenan Rockmore and Kel Kimble, our on-screen mischievous misadventures earned us a Favorite TV Show award at the Kids' Choice Awards in 1998.

The powers that be—the network, the producers, the writers—desperately wanted to turn us into a comedy duo like Laurel and Hardy or Lewis and Martin, the straight guy with an annoying but love-able sidekick. Back then, I was a big Martin Lawrence fan and pulled from what I saw him do on his show, *Martin*. He executed the perfect balance of straight-man frustration with ignorant hijinx to the max. Martin was a master of physicality and displaying on his face exactly what everyone around him—and watching him at home—was think-ing. I watched my cousins laugh really hard at *Martin*, and I respected their senses of humor so much because it seemed like when something struck them as funny, it struck them as really, really funny. I wanted to hit people's funny bones like that.

Kel and I enjoyed working together and performing comedy, so the grueling workload on both *All That* and *Kenan & Kel* didn't bother us. I was grinding, with my best buddy, my brother. But it was always important to us that people saw us as individuals; Kel and I didn't want to be considered an "act" and unable to work without each other. We always made sure that everybody knew our first and last names, and not just called us our team name.

But life was fun. We started getting invited to the dopest things, like the NBA All-Star weekend. We partied for sure, but we also got up at the crack of dawn to do the Saturday-morning kids' version while everyone else was passed out in their hotel rooms. It was a paradise situation. I was excited to wake up in the morning, like, the birds were chirping. *Oh, it's a brand-new day, time to go to work!*

The rare moments we weren't working, we lived at Jerry's Deli, a hot spot for young Hollywood at the time. We were adults now, but we were still underage, so it was less sex, drugs, and rock 'n' roll, more corned beef on rye. If there was illegal stuff going on around me, I was blissfully ignorant. I think it was a really good thing we started out in Orlando; it kept us humble.

When production moved to LA in 1996, *All That*'s producers added a few new cast members. Amanda Bynes was only ten years old when she arrived on set, but her star took off quickly, largely due to her sketch "Ask Ashley," about a preteen who offered blunt advice from her bedroom. That was Amanda's missile to the moon. She was adorable and had a ginormous range of talent. She was the best, man; we were very close. She was like all of our little sister, and we were all very protective of her, just like we were of Katrina. Katrina used to be our baby, but now she was starting to grow up, and it's like when parents don't have a kid in diapers anymore, and they're like, *What's happening? Let's have another baby!* When Amanda came in, we got a new wee one to nurture and spoil. We had to watch out for our little ones.

Amanda was the sweetest, happiest girl, and she loved to laugh. She was an explosion of bright innocence and joy. She was funny whether the cameras were rolling or not. She was an old soul, it was almost like she'd made the decision at that young of an age to be the next Carol Burnett. I remember she was so knowledgeable about Lucille Ball's comedy style. I connected with her because she was laser-focused like me and had a very sweet, supportive family, too. Unfortunately, some leeches sent her down a dark path. When she went left for a little while, we all were sad. I cared about her, and I still do. She's good people.

Danny Tamberelli was also a new addition to the *All That* crew. He was in the original *The Mighty Ducks* and *The Adventures of Pete & Pete*, another popular Nickelodeon program at the time. He turned out to be very silly and his humor was ridiculous, right up our alley. He was younger than us guys, so we hazed him a little bit. But then we started kicking it and he became one of my dearest buddies. We both live in New York now, and he's a prolific bass player and gives me free guitar lessons. He's dope.

Last but not least, *All That* was blessed with the talent of Nick Cannon. Nick was the comic who warmed up our live audiences before the start of each taping. Not long after, he joined the cast as a principal player. I thought at first he was just a young player, as in "playa," trying to break into it with his looks because he was a handsome kid. But people got past his looks because he was dead serious about comedy. He was only sixteen at the time, driving himself back and forth from his home in San Diego to LA to do stand-up comedy. He was talented.

So he had that hustle, and he took the opportunity to warm up the *All That* audience and ran with it and turned himself into the Nick Cannon we know today. You gotta respect that. But as far as the showbiz stuff, Nick drank the corny Hollywood Kool-Aid early. Back in the day, he wore a lot of rayon shirts and Hush Puppies. He bought himself a used Range Rover immediately so he could play the part. If he was going to grab coffee with a producer or director, he wanted to pull up in the Rover, not his old Beamer. Nick was a ladies' man for sure, but I didn't think he was gonna turn out to be Captain Splash around town necessarily and have a dozen kids. He's a madman; I don't know if he's gonna stop. There might be a petition soon.

Nick and Kel were very close in the beginning, and Nick would often crash at Kel's place near mine in Beverly Hills, instead of driving back home to San Diego. Kel had a girlfriend that was hanging around a lot, and one night, he left Nick outside for hours while they got busy. Nick sat in his car all night. I happened to randomly be coming back from a night out at five a.m. and drove right past him. Nick spotted me, followed me home, and pulled into my garage behind me. I thought I was getting carjacked, but no, it was just Nick, exhausted, stiff, and bleary-eyed.

"What's up?" I said.

"Kel left me outside all night."

"For real, bro? Maybe he fell asleep or something. You can come crash." I was single but had an extra bedroom. "Man, just take that bedroom so you don't have to drive back and forth." And that's how Nick and I became roommates for a year. We had a brotherly kind of relationship. We were both young and in the game and needed to support each other. *All That* and *Kenan & Kel* were both shooting on Sunset and Argyle, so when the lease was up, I decided I wanted to be closer to set. Nick and I got a crib in the middle of Laurel Canyon. I was intrigued with living up there because I had seen so many classic, cool movies that were shot in the Hollywood Hills, from *Rebel Without a Cause* to *Magnolia*. We didn't have a view of diddly, but that was okay. It was available, in our price range, and the landlord was willing to rent it to couple of nineteen-year-olds. Done deal. It was fun, like a little tree house, plus it had a cheesy wooden hot tub. I had never seen anything quite like it. It was small, like one bedroom and a half, about the size of a closet. That was Nick's sleeping space. I can't technically call it a room—that would be a lie, and Thompsons don't lie—but he made it work. He worked all day, then would come home and go straight into his "room" and turn it into a studio. That's when Nick first started making beats. That's where he taught himself how to make music. And we became brothers for life.

We were so proud of ourselves for living in a house. It was the best of times—our moment to be kings. We had all the freedom in the world. If we wanted to watch *Half Baked* every single day and twice on Sundays, we could, and we did. I no longer had my mom monitoring my programs or looking over my shoulder. I had a house, a car, two jobs, and then, soon, my first starring role: in the movie version of *Good Burger.*

I wish we could say we were intimately involved in the creative process around it, but back then, they just handed us a script and told us where to be and when. Our producers were like, "We're turning 'Good Burger' into a movie." We said, "Great," and my one question was, "What character will I play?" Because it didn't seem like Lester Oaks, construction worker, had the legs to carry half a movie. So they made me a regular person named Dexter Reed who could gel with Kel's crazy character, Ed.

We had Josh with us, Sinbad, Abe Vigoda, Ron Lester, Shar Jackson; it felt like a family. Being around Abe was crazy good because I was a big fan of *The Godfather* and *Barney Miller.* I was over the moon. I couldn't believe Fish/Salvatore Tessio wanted to be in our little movie, but Abe was game for anything. We were making fun of an old guy for being old, and he was cool with it. We had him running around in an insane asylum, and Abe really committed to the work and the character. A total pro.

Sinbad, forget it. He was another one of my first go-tos because he did clean comedy. I was a big fan when I saw him do his *Brain Damaged* comedy taping. He did it at Morehouse College in Atlanta. I remember being a kid sitting in the balcony, watching this guy, like, *Man, he's great. I would love to do something like that.* You know what I mean? To be able to entertain a large crowd like that, you know, and make it look so effortless was really cool to watch and see. And also to see a little bit of Hollywood in Atlanta early on.

So it was super surreal meeting him because on top of being insanely hilarious, he was nice and mentor-ish. Everything I could dream up, he was. His trailer was really nice; he'd made sure of that in his contract. That was the best advice he gave me: to make sure my contracts were straight. Mostly he just led by example. He came in, did his work, had his kids with him. Not a whole lot of people can hold a crowd like Sinbad, whether at the Kennedy Center for Performing Arts or in Las Vegas in the middle of the afternoon.

Oh, and let's not forget Carmen Electra, who played Roxanne and was the hottest woman on the planet. Every morning she was dropped off by her then-boyfriend B-Real from the hip-hop group Cypress Hill. To see his Chevrolet Dually drop down to the ground and watch Carmen shimmy outta the passenger side and catwalk over to us other slobs milling around on set, well, it was jaw-dropping. We were cartoon characters—our eyes popped out of our heads, our tongues rolled out like a red carpet, and steam blew out of our ears. Respectfully, of course.

While *Good Burger* wasn't the first movie I'd been on, it was the first one where I was so high on the call sheet. For the first time, I had my own trailer; it was old and run-down, but it had a bed in it. For napping! I was a grown-up, for real. I remember saying out loud to myself, sprawled out on my bed like a starfish, "This is boss."

It was also the first time I had an on-screen kiss, and it should have been my last. My love interest, Mo'Nique, was played by *Moesha* star Shar Jackson. Now, I knew I was no Blair Underwood or Denzel Washington. I was eighteen by this point, so it wasn't like I hadn't kissed a girl. I had no problem with the ladies in real life, but on-screen I just wasn't that guy. This was forced kissing, from someone who you don't know if they even like you. But we had to do it regardless. I practiced on the back of my hand in my trailer. I was so nervous, even though it was a surface-level, plain-as-it-could-have-possibly-been kiss. I was like, *Yep, I'm fine with that. Just a peck and, Lord, let it just be over fast.* I didn't think it was gonna be a whole lot of tongue action—there was no sucking or lip biting—but I definitely didn't think it was gonna be as chapped-lip-on-chapped-lip as it was. It was just pursed lip on pursed lip. My lips were super wrinkled and uncomfortable. After each take they'd say, "Maybe hold it a little longer," and then we'd do the exact same thing. By take four, I was like, *Let's bring somebody else in to kiss Shar because I don't know if she wants this from me.* I knew she had a boyfriend. It was too much for me.

I was not used to making out or kissing in front of people, like, deliberately. I didn't grow up playing Spin the Bottle. You got the action where you got the action, and usually it was hidden behind a tree and it was between just the two of you. But it was an innocent kiss, and Shar was a sweetheart about it. She was very gentle with me.

None of my on-screen kisses have ever been any good. I've never gotten into a *now, that was sexy* kind of feeling. When I look back at it, they're all just weird pecks because I'm not the open-mouth-with-strangers guy. Or even the friends-who-make-work-awkward type.

While we were shooting for three months, we could feel that insane energy, and we knew we were in our golden era. We were evolving as actors, pushing our limits and taking ourselves seriously as performers and businessmen. We'd gotten a movie based off a sketch my brother from another mother created, based on our senses of humor.

We had so much fun traveling all over the country to promote *Good Burger*—from the 'hood to the Hamptons. But my favorite memory was flying to the Toronto International Film Festival, and we just so happened to be on the same plane with Phil Hartman, the late legendary impressionist/actor from *Saturday Night Live*. When the seat belt sign went off and people were stretching their legs, we stood up, and he came around and started shooting the breeze with us. We were up in the clouds, literally and figuratively. It was so trippy.

The whole *Good Burger* experience made it that more clear to me: it was undeniable that this is what I was supposed to be doing with my life.

We wanted *Good Burger* to be good and well received, sure, but we had no idea it would be so beloved and oft-quoted and become a comedy cult classic. That was the icing on the cake. Once we were done shooting, we weirdly thought maybe that was kind of the end of the good times. Little did we know.

With *Good Burger* under our belts and after six years on two shows, Kel and I were officially burnt-out and running on autopilot. We and some of the other *All That* castmates were also getting older, and fear started to settle in—we were afraid of being typecast as child actors for the rest of our lives. None of us wanted to do that Ralph Macchio dance of being pigeonholed as child actors. I could see how Jaleel White, one of our close buddies, struggled to distance himself from Steve Urkel and pursue different opportunities. Luckily, he was smart enough to earn a degree at UCLA and cultivate some really smart, business-minded relationships with industry people and not starve to death or be reliant on SAG unemployment. I always kept Jaleel in mind after *Good Burger*; his situation echoed so loud with me because he was such a talented, good dude. If he were an asshole, I'd be like, *Well, that's probably why you're not working.* But he was one of the nicest people in the world. And so insanely funny.

Jaleel was able to survive that. But three years after I started *All That*, teen star Jonathan Brandis, the guy we all aspired to be like when we first started out back in Orlando, killed himself. It was a huge blow to me. I was a big fan of his and always admired his dedication to his craft; Jonathan was goals to me. I really wondered if Jonathan was depressed about being stuck in his child stardom, of always being that recognized face, and couldn't find a way out. That haunted me.

When he took his life, it made me really sad. I don't know why he did it, but it led to a lot of deep thinking for me. About that double-edged sword of dedicating 1,000 percent to a job like acting. You want to be fully committed to each role, but the nature of the profession can easily consume you and distort reality. Jonathan's tragic death put so much into perspective for me, and I realized I shouldn't worry about comparing my road to success with other people's. It was important that I remember to follow my own path and what was for me was for me.

Even though I was concerned about being pigeonholed and about my future as an actor, I was still so grateful to be working and understood it was important to give my all, every time. I was aware that other people's livelihoods depended on me showing up and doing a good job every day—the *All That* crew was pulling thirteen-hour shifts, seven days per week, and I wasn't going to complicate their jobs by not doing mine.

By this time, I had started seeing a change in Kel. He was jaded. He was so over it. He was really going through it and got funky with everybody, which posed a huge problem for me. He was experiencing a growing pain I just wasn't going through. He wanted something new, different; he wanted to be off Nickelodeon and on to his adult superstardom or to be a rapper, his true passion.

At first Kel didn't direct his ire in my direction. He couldn't dismiss me so easily; we were tethered together professionally and personally. But I knew it would eventually come my way. I knew I wasn't going to be the one person who could escape the wrath of a frustrated individual. As much as we tried to have individual careers, we were a unit at that point. And we were very aware of the stories of comedy duos like Abbott and Costello breaking up and not really being able to get work without each other. We didn't want to have a breakup story. But that's exactly what happened: Kel and I went our separate ways.

SEVEN

Behind the Scenes:
Black Is Still Beautiful

There's no question my parents and their iron fists are a big reason I kept my head screwed on straight and held it above water after getting famous so young. But there were other angels on my shoulders guiding me the whole way—the strong, successful Black men who mentored me during the most impressionable times of my life, in actual, real, waking life, not just watching them on my favorite sitcoms.

Let's start with my big brother, Kerwin. I was kind of forced on him, but to his credit, he never minded it. He was my first buddy and my main man. It's easier to go through life when you know that you have a ride or die who loves you unconditionally. He had a big personality and a big heart. Not a big personality in the sense of *Hey, everybody gather round.* He was a powerful presence, a firstborn child with natural leadership qualities. If he was going to be in the band, he was going to be drum major. If he was going to be on the football team, he was going to be the quarterback. He was outgoing, an Aries. He had a lot of friends and a lot of interests, from sports to the chess and debate clubs. On top of all that, he was really smart, much smarter than me.

Sure, there were times we fought, especially when Kerwin went through puberty and wanted to go out and do his own thing. There was a brief period when he was finally able to borrow the car, so he left me home a lot and didn't take me to football and basketball games. But then Kerwin realized younger brothers were chick magnets and he had to do too much work on his own, and before you know it, I was back by his side.

Kerwin and I get closer every single day. We're so darn close we have a secret language. Most people text, "Hi, how you doing"—basic stuff. Kerwin and I don't text that way. We have a special form of communication that is only dialogue from our favorite movies. We'll go back and forth exchanging lines, and we'll finish the scene, and that will be the end of it; we're good. And somehow we know exactly what the conversation was really about. It's so much fun and quite touching . . . to us . . . though it's always baffled and annoyed our significant others. We got a lot of, "Can't you just ask your brother to bring the turkey and stuffing over like a normal person? You guys are so weird."

When Kerwin dipped out for college, that left a huge void. Luckily, another mentor stepped up right around that time. When we were younger, my brother and I had played instruments in the Youth Ensemble of Atlanta, led by prolific theater icon Freddie Hendricks. Flash forward: in eleventh grade I transferred to Tri-Cities, my local public high school, around the corner from my house. As luck would have it, Freddie had become the acting teacher at the high school, and once I joined the drama department, I thrived. I could not have been in a better, warmer nest. I found my people. I started learning about the pedigree of Freddie and all his actor friends in the Black theater scene and at the 14th Street Playhouse in Atlanta. They had this bond that just washed down on us by watching them. This motto of *If I got it, then you got it* kept echoing through their conversations. Everything was all of ours. It was a great mentality to grow up with and was great training for an ensemble-minded person like myself.

• • •

GETTING THE CHANCE TO HANG OUT WITH THOMAS JEFFERSON Byrd, Freddie's godson and an actor in many of Spike Lee's joints, including *Get on the Bus*, *He Got Game*, and *Bamboozled*, was *incredible*. He was one of those amazing character actor types trained to do anything under the sun. He took being an artist very seriously, and to Thomas, it was all about the craft. Whenever Spike needed a real actor, Thomas was one of those guys. And that's a precious thing.

While I was under Freddie's tutelage, Thomas was in between movies and would stop by our rehearsals and chill with us. We would all ride home together, and I'd listen to the adults having conversations in the back seat. Thomas was a movie star but also a real individual. You'd think he would have traveled around in a Mercedes, but he was fine to ride with us in whatever broke-down Nissan us kids had. Sadly, Thomas was shot and killed while walking near his home in Southwest Atlanta in 2020. I'm so grateful I got so much time with him and he taught me so much. The biggest lesson I learned from Thomas was that being an actor is not a forever job. There are going to be times when you're really searching or in between and trying to maintain balance.

Freddie showed us what a realistic goal looked like, and it wasn't about the money. It was about being good—even if we were starving artists at first—and we all wanted to be good. We learned that you'll never know how your checks are gonna roll in this business, but that it doesn't really matter. If you're getting paid often enough to sustain life, that's living the dream. That became the mentality of all of us students and brought us closer.

My high school theater group was very dramatic and serious. It was so funny because when I wasn't in school, I was at Nickelodeon doing the silliest comedy ever. Not with Freddie. According to the book *Black Acting Methods*, the Hendricks Method was about "empowered authorship, musical bravado, spirituality, ensemble building, activism, effusive reverence of Black culture, and devising, often sans script." We wrote our own plays and workshopped monologues and performed hypersensitive material about teen violence, teen AIDS, drug addiction, South African apartheid. We were the first students to do *The Color Purple*, for cryin' out loud. I definitely was given the lines that would lift the audience from the heaviness, but comedy was not the point or the priority. Freddie's drama school usually won state competitions.

You can't buy the training and life lessons I got from Freddie. All of his friends came from that prolific Black theater era. Laurence Fishburne, Samuel L. Jackson, Wesley Snipes—they were all onstage together in New York and in the South, and we got to hear all of the stories. I remember we had political activist Stokely Carmichael, now known as Kwame Ture, one of the Freedom Riders, come speak to us at one point. He was such a huge motivator.

If not necessarily revolutionary, they were all conscious and aware of certain ceiling placements and systematic oppression on the Black man in America. Take your pick—policing, disparity in education, the lack of diversity of NFL ownership or amongst Fortune 500 CEOs. They were also shining examples of the reality that there's no guarantee you're going to be rich and famous as an actor. It wasn't about that. It was being good at the craft and having the respect of your peers that would keep you working. Being a dependable performer. And also feeding that performance itch because we can't sit around too long without pouring out some sort of version of what we're taking in. Performers are sponges. We reflect life. If it builds up without us being able to let it out in some sort of controlled fashion, it'll just explode at parties.

I was being taught inside secrets by legends. That obviously had a huge impact on who I became as a comedian and can be seen a lot in my work on *SNL*. My first real comedy mentor was Steve Harvey, after I landed my first real acting gig on his sitcom *The Steve Harvey Show*, about a former failed R & B singer who takes a job as a high school teacher and has to deal with precocious teens. This time overlapped with the tail end of *All That* and *Kenan & Kel*, and Steve's guidance and advice was especially timely. Doling out advice to his young cast like Yoda, both he and his iconic costar Cedric the Entertainer were so helpful in terms of honing my comedy. With these guys, it was all about elevating the craft. From them, I learned how to squeeze out laughs past the words—get your line out, but if you don't get a laugh, exit the scene with whatever you can do physically to get that laugh.

One night, I followed Steve to his car; I was annoyingly imposing. Steve pulled out of his parking spot, and I waved to him to stop. He rolled down the window, and the smooth drawl of Lou Rawls wafted into my earholes.

"What you listening to, man?" I asked, trying to make conversation but having no idea what to say. "You like hip-hop?"

"I don't listen to hip-hop, son. I'm a grown man."

That was a big wake-up moment for me. Onstage, Steve was so energetic and happy, but he was not my little play buddy. He was a *real* adult. There was a big difference between performing and real life. That stuck with me, as did another piece of advice he shared with me more than once: *Take every job they offer you.* That line stayed with me the rest of my career.

With Steve, from day one, it was no nonsense. It was tough love from him: do your job, because you don't even know how hard it was for me and the others before you. Steve was homeless at one point. And then here I come, stopping him from leaving the lot after a long day, telling him to roll down the window, and hanging on it, as if I got something special to say. And all I ask him is, "What you listening to? DMX?"

In Black culture, the best men are very serious in making sure the young boys in their world aren't acting up and are on their best behavior. Especially guys that come from country origins, like Steve. They're sticklers for discipline and absolutely keeping an eye out to make sure you're not messing up. I remember Steve and Cedric mentoring my buddy Merlin Santana, who played Romeo on the show, a lot, and trying to bring him under their wings. Like me, he was a child actor emerging into his adult years. He was a really, really good person, but he was an LA city kid who was dealing with one foot in the street and one foot in Hollywood. Steve and Ced would encourage him to focus on the show and stay out of trouble. They were doing that for all of us.

Unfortunately, Merlin caught a bad one. While sitting in a car on Crenshaw Boulevard in November 2002, he was shot in the back of the head. He was only twenty-six.

I think about how grateful I am to have made it so far, knock on wood. I never put myself into too many situations where I didn't really know where I was or that there was possibly danger. I wasn't out of bounds; I knew where the safety zones were. I wasn't exposed to a bunch of drug users, either. It's not a big thing in the Black entertainment community to be doing coke or smoking crack or popping pills. And if you did that, it was very much behind closed doors. I was also on Nickelodeon, a kids' network, so it was another *Purple Rain* thing: if I'm not allowed to watch *Purple Rain* yet, I sure as Shirley can't be on the streets around a bunch of cocaine-using people. If I went to somebody's house party and there were a bunch of drugs on the table, I never saw that. Ignorance was bliss for me.

The Steve Harvey Show was a wholesome environment. Steve always talked about his mom being in the church all his life, just like my mom, and I found comfort and familiarity in that. Although Steve was focused on work, that didn't mean that Steve didn't know how to have a good time. He liked to be out and about. Steve wanted to celebrate his successes in the moment (as opposed to waiting for the end of the season like most shows), so after every taping, Steve and the cast would go to Denzel Washington's restaurant Georgia on Melrose Avenue in West Hollywood.

Life was always fun. Once the Nickelodeon shows moved to LA, we started bumping into the who's who of Black Hollywood: Queen Latifah, the Wayans brothers, Tichina Arnold, Brian McKnight, Mike Epps. Back in those days, there were definitely certain parties or certain nights where it was Black night at a club like Mirabelle, a spot decorated like a boat. Once you got into that rotation, then you started really seeing everybody. We all went to the same restaurants, like Roscoe's Chicken & Waffles, and held after-parties at Black-owned clubs like Shark Bar, where NFL star Keyshawn Johnson was a major investor. It was a tight circle of working Black faces.

The best part about this clique was that everybody had each other's backs. The stereotype of the Black man missing in the family and society in general is rampant, but in the industry, Black Hollywood was a very tight-knit group. We were always going to each other's birthday parties and baby showers and just supporting each other. Amongst ourselves, we cultivated an environment of safety, the same collection of Black illuminati faces. We were a family.

It was also the golden age of Black sitcoms—*Martin, Living Single, The Fresh Prince of Bel-Air*—and I remember visiting everyone's sets and wandering around their sound stages. We went to *Moesha* and *The Wayans Bros.* to kick it. I did episodes of *The Parkers* and *Sister, Sister*, and LL Cool J's show *In the House*. I'll never forget the time I bumped into Jamie Foxx backstage on his eponymous TV show. I hadn't met him before, but a buddy of mine introduced me to him when he was leaving his dressing room and going out to do his next scene. He stopped without hesitation. "Hey, man," Jamie said to me, "you got all the talent in the world."

I couldn't believe it. That's crazy coming from Jamie Foxx. He probably could have said that to every kid he passed, but it really stuck with me. The fact that he took the time to say something encouraging to me is what I held on to. Whether or not I believed he believed I had all the talent in the world didn't matter; it was that he did something small that made a big difference for me . . . I took that extra blanket of confidence to every performance after that, every audition. Someone who I thoroughly looked up to thought I had all the talent in the world. I took that mentality and ran with it.

There are always going to be times when you're up against someone for a role, but my early role models taught me by example that there's room for everybody and there's more power in locking arms and moving forward than the crabs-in-a-bucket BS, trying to pull each other down because you want your moment. I tell my girls this all the time when they bicker or get competitive with each other. They're young and new to all of this, but they'll get to the age soon when they realize nobody has your back like your sister.

So let's root for each other and hope for the best. We can all chase the dream together. And that's a beautiful thing.

EIGHT

The Huggable Cutie

I'll never forget the time Chris Farley guest starred on *All That*. I loved working with Angelique on the cooking bit "Cooking with Randy and Mandy," but after season two she left the show and I had the sketch to myself. When the producers told me at table read that Chris was going to cameo as the Chicago Ketchup Chef on the renamed "Cooking with Randy," I think I fell out of my chair. It would be just me and Chris Farley, getting messy and being silly.

On extra-special taping days, when guest stars would come on the show, the cast would stare out the window, nose to the glass, waiting for guests like Brandy or Aaliyah to pop out of their black town cars. They seemed as important as the president. The day Farley arrived felt like the Pope himself was blessing our humble studio. The whole larger-than-life thing wasn't just advertising.

Farley busted into the studio knowing exactly what he was going to do, and rehearsal was not part of that plan. The crew brought in a treasure chest–sized frosted chocolate cake for the Chicago Ketchup Chef to ruin with, you guessed it, ketchup. The director told Chris not to touch the cake on the first take, because there was only one. But if someone told Chris Farley not to do something, he was going to do it anyway. I knew this. My mom knew this. Everyone on the planet knew this—except for the director. I knew Farley was going to go overboard from the way he shook my hand at the top of the sketch, like a wrestler trying to low-key let his opponent know, *I got this*. I was just happy to be along for the ride, as you can tell from my poorly hidden smile in the sketch. Farley was nose-deep in the cake before the director had a chance to yell, "Cut!" Literally minutes after we met, we were hurling chocolate and ketchup at each other. And just like that, he pulled an Elvis and left the building. He passed away less than a year later.

When I heard about his death, I remember needing to take a few minutes in my dressing room to collect myself. He was a true master. Getting to work so closely with him in his prime was like getting to play one-on-one with Jordan, pre–*Space Jam*. Farley was gone, but his presence stuck with me for a long time.

Farley was a huge influence, pun intended. Nobody on television looked or acted like he did. The hefty actors, like John Belushi and John Candy, who came before him were cool, but Farley was my favorite. He weighed about three hundred pounds yet could do cartwheels, and smash through tables and get right back up. At the time, I didn't associate his death with obesity. I associated it with drug abuse only, as opposed to unchecked excess, like the whole bag of not-taking-care-of-yourself.

Being in the public eye, I've been on a very clear display of healthy living and unhealthy living. When I first started out in showbiz, Farley was a role model—to see a bigger guy be so comfortable with his size and use it to his strength was inspiring to a teenage chubster like myself. Like Farley, my body and its size is part of my legacy. I've built my career around being the "funny, fat Black comic."

My nickname as a kid was Chubs. It came from this one specific jerk, and it used to irk the you-know-what out of me. He thought calling me that was cute, almost affectionate, in a tough-love kind of way. But it really got under my skin. His fat-shaming didn't make me go home and look in the mirror with self-loathing per se, but it stayed with me for a long time.

I was on the smaller side until I hit puberty. My growth was so stunted—I was still five foot flat in tenth grade—that I had to give myself thyroid shots in the thigh so I wouldn't look like a bowling ball with eyes. I absolutely hated doing those shots; the needle scared the bejesus outta me, but it worked. I shot up ten inches in due time.

It didn't help that I grew up on fast food, which, back then, was still considered real food. Eating at McDonald's wasn't considered a shameful secret; it was a delightful treat. I started many a mornin' with a sausage biscuit, and that would be a very happy day. Double quarter pounders with cheese for lunch? That was my jam. When I was a kid, Burger King, Wendy's, and Red Lobster were all in close proximity, and that was a recipe for disaster (not to mention heart disease). We were latchkey kids, so we ate sugary cereals like Lucky Charms and Fruity Pebbles for breakfast because the adults had to get to work and didn't have the time to make more nutritious, healthy meals. Lunch was processed meat on white bread with Miracle Whip. After school, we might come home alone and eat a stack of Kraft American cheese singles and a giant bag of Doritos before dinner. Dinner was often processed TV dinners or frozen fish sticks. In hindsight, being latchkey wasn't really a good idea. It took a while for everybody to wake up to the fact that you're not supposed to send middle schoolers home by themselves. Today, everybody would be kidnapped. Everybody would just be dead.

To the best of my recollection, nobody drank water back then, either. Back in my day, if you were thirsty at school, you had to wait until the bell rang, then stand in a long line at a water fountain behind a bunch of germy kids with sticky fingers and runny noses. You best not put your mouth on that spout, or you might get a slap on the back of your head and crack your tooth. And there was a strict time enforcement. Gulp as much water down as you could from a lukewarm thin stream within about three seconds, then move on, son. Everyone had to get to their next class and needed a turn. They couldn't be late because you were hogging the fountain.

Water just wasn't a thing yet. We sucked Capri Suns out of straws poked into baggy pouches, and literally drank the Kool-Aid because of a commercial in which a cheerful, cherry-colored jug of juice audaciously crashed through a wall and sang a radical catchphrase of "Oh yeah!" In my house, a pitcher of Kool-Aid called for one and a half cups of sugar, minimum. On hot summer days, we'd crack open a cooler and grab an ice-cold Coca-Cola or Dr Pepper, dripping wet from ice, gulp it down, and go, "Aaaaaah." I don't ever remember hearing anyone tell us not to or use the word "diabetes" in casual conversation.

The more I focused on acting, the less physical activity—like playing sports—I did, and the higher my weight climbed. As I got more successful, I went through a phase of *Oh, I can afford to eat anything I want, and I can almost eat anything I want because I'm young and I have a giant appetite.* But my metabolism was slow—I didn't even know what that meant, or I guess I didn't care because I was busy working. It just wasn't top of mind. Unlike so many women in showbiz, nobody ever told me I needed to lose weight in my early days. My survival and my success in life weren't dependent on my physical appearance, necessarily. I had a job, and I always had girlfriends. As far as wanting to stay in shape or be sexy or whatever, I didn't feel the pressure of, *How am I gonna stand out in this world of billions?*

In fact, in my career, from the start, my weight was almost celebrated. Being the big boy gave me a big turkey leg up in the biz, starting with *D2: The Mighty Ducks*, then starring as *Fat Albert*—an absolute dream at the time—up to *SNL*, which has always had big guys in the cast—Belushi, Farley, Bobby Moynihan (the sweetest person walking). For so many years after that, I embraced my nickname and my body because I was like, *Well, that's just my body frame, what can I do about it?* It took me a while to snap out of it and realize that stereotyping myself wasn't good for my self-esteem and, more important, not dropping dead.

On *All That*, everyone was designated a role during sketch casting: Kel was the smooth talker, Josh was the heartthrob, and I was the huggable cutie, and I was aight with that. It was never my desire to be the ladies' man. The girls that everybody wanted to date started as genuine friends first. I was friends with everybody, and some turned into admirers, and there you go. I got to make out with whoever liked me. Later as an adult and a bachelor, when I would need to strike up a conversation and make good first impressions, I was lucky enough to have a lot of things in my arsenal. Maybe I didn't have a six-pack, but girls would recognize my face, or they could tell that I wasn't necessarily broke. So I put all those cards on the table first without having to be the guy that could just walk up to any lady and strike up a conversation. Getting attention from women wasn't a problem, so that didn't motivate me to watch what I ate. In fact, it might have inadvertently given me permission to be even more gluttonous.

MY ON-SCREEN ROLES DIDN'T HELP, EITHER. ALL THE FOOD I'VE HAD to eat on camera over the years, dating back to "Cooking with Randy and Mandy" on *All That*, probably took three months off of my life. When I filmed *Heavyweights*, a comedy about plump kids learning to lose weight at fat camp, we took it upon ourselves to pig out. We considered it method acting. I had my sixteenth birthday on that movie, and that was my first wake-up call that maybe I was unhealthy, because I was cast specifically for being overweight. It's not like I got a fat suit to wear. It was all me. Up to that point I didn't think I was super overweight; I just thought I was stocky. I was living the dream—my career was bubbling, and I was getting paid to be around super-successful guys like Judd Apatow, who wrote *Heavyweights*, and act alongside legit stars like Paul Feig, Ben Stiller, Peter Berg, and Shaun Weiss, my castmate from *D2*. The star stocky kid in the movie, Aaron Schwartz, is not only a close friend to this day, but his body is now super shredded.

Heavyweights was the epitome of those cowboy comedy days. We were filming in a camp amongst the trees in North Carolina and, during our off time, hanging out in the parking lot of the Holiday Inn motel we'd taken over. I need to mention that this movie set was the historical site of my inaugural wacky tobaccy smoking, like, for real. Then we'd go to Taco Bell and go nuts. Maybe it was subliminally the munchies, but I felt like I *deserved* to crush Taco Supremes and burritos all summer—I was aware of the movie title and concept. But my ignorance diluted a more important message: *Hey, you're starting to typecast yourself as a heavy person. Heavyweights* would probably never get greenlit today. Yes, it had a message: the kids stuck together and triumphed being themselves, but nowhere in it was anyone trying to get healthy or take care of themselves. None of that. I don't think Judd wrote it to be mean. It was funny at the time, and society's sensibilities were different then. There were tons of other inappropriate teen movies, like *Porky's* and *The Last American Virgin*. So yes, let's send a bunch of fat kids to camp—it'll be hilarious! As opposed to, *Hey, this might not be the best thing for the psyche of a young person.*

Just like with the fried chicken commercial, I allowed myself to be exploited a little, this time for cheap laughs. There was a little workout uniform we all had to wear, and I was self-conscious about it because it accentuated my belly and butt. It was small on purpose, one of those outfits that made the chubby kids look super-plus chubby. I kind of disassociated from the situation. Instead of saying to myself, *This is unhealthy both physically and mentally,* I convinced myself that it wasn't happening to *me,* Kenan; I was playing a part, and it was happening to my character. I was an actor playing the role of a chubby kid in a comedy, and this was how I fit into it.

I'll never forget when I first read the Superdude sketch on *All That.* I was so excited to play a superhero. Then I realized I'd have to wear tights. At the time, I was self-conscious about my upper parts. I spent a month running, lifting, and swimming laps in vats of green slime to get into true Superdude shape. Just kidding—I took steroids. It was the mid-'90s. Everyone was doing it. There's a reason why I've never really had my shirt off in a movie or on a TV show. I did it later in my career, in the movie *Wieners,* a road-trip movie about a bunch of guys who drive across the country in a Wiener Wagon to get revenge on a talk show host. I only agreed to it because I didn't want to leave my buddy Zach Levi out in the cold alone. He had to do an embarrassing stripper routine that he never really signed up for. None of us ever really signed up to put on Daisy Duke shorts. Even if you're a comedian who happens to be in shape, you're still not thinking, *I can't wait to jump into a Speedo and show off my junk!* When it came down to that moment, Zach was like, "Man, you guys can't leave me hanging." I bit the bullet and took my shirt off. But I hated it. I was so outta shape. In my mind, it would've been better to have my shirt on.

I was at my heaviest during my early *SNL* years. I was lying around and going to rehearsal and eating late and not necessarily working out. And then I hit my bottom. One of my favorite random sketches—I played a cannibal up for parole doing the *Shawshank Redemption* speech—I was at my heaviest moment, and that's always hard to rewatch. Surprisingly, the first person to start me on the right path was Lorne Michaels. Actually it was my mom; she'd been trying for years but I didn't want to hear it at the time. At the very beginning of *SNL,* he encouraged me to take care of my body. "It's kind of all you have," he told me. It was his way of encouraging me to live healthier. Basically saying, *Live healthier.* He never shunned me or ever brought it up again, like, *Hey, you never took my advice.* I wasn't surprised when he said that to me; I was more, *Aw, shoot, my slip is showing.* I wasn't as fortified as I'd thought, as far as presenting Kenan to the world was concerned. There was a leak in the dam, enough for someone who cared to say something about it.

Anytime I went to dinner with Lorne, it'd be at a healthier place, and he set an example that way. People follow good examples sometimes, even if they don't or can't hear it in word form. Lorne is a machine. He works out, he goes to his doctors, and they hate him because he's so healthy at his age, and they're his age and they're in worse shape, and they're doctors! He watches his diet because he likes to fit into his Gucci sweaters. His style is Midwestern business-casual gentleman, always presentable 24/7, so he can go to a high-end museum opening on the spur of the moment. *SNL* was always wonderful about supporting me, especially the wardrobe people. Those guys were so loving and positive and never judged me. They tailored my clothes. They didn't make comments, just adjustments.

I took Lorne's words to heart, ultimately, because it seemed like he cared about me, but the ball was in my court. Me living healthy wouldn't change anything for him; it was for me and that was a light bulb moment.

My weight had gone up and down a few times. I tried all kinds of fat burner pills, not exactly the Anna Nicole Smith kind, nothing crazy that would make me holler, "TrimSpa, baby!" More like the booster kind from GNC. But they don't boost much of anything from dormancy. The answer would always boil down to, you can take as many pills as you want, but if you're still lying around and you're eating bad, you might not like the result.

After I got married, and we started nesting, I kind of let myself go. In the early part of a relationship, when you're just hooking up, you still try really hard, and you still really care about your appearance. Once you're deep into that relationship, you can get a little lazier, unless you have a micro-dick or something. At the beginning, I always feel like I'm a valuable part of the relationship and feel confident about being nekkid with a lady. But my theory is, the more intimate you get, the more self-conscious you get about your body. Especially when you start being around each other in the daytime and you're not drunk. You're just in your undies, no T-shirt, and showing a lot of crack. It takes real love for somebody to look at you and see that as attractive. That's real intimacy.

There came a point with my weight that I couldn't deny what I was seeing anymore—a puffed individual. The turning point finally came when my wife pointed out that my pillowcases had turned colors. I was so unhealthy, I was sweating at night and staining the sheets. Whatever was secreting out of my body in the wee hours, it wasn't good. You should not be neck sweating to death in your sleep. It was a gradual wake-up call. Too gradual, I would say.

For me, diet and exercise were the only options. I knew I couldn't keep eating three or four hot dogs at a time, or a double cheeseburger at Denny's at three a.m. There's no reason for you to eat two chicken sandwiches at every meal. You can't just eat everything. I ended up cutting out red meat and soda, officially, forever. It gave me the boost I needed to not overly restrict my diet.

When it came to moving my body, I just wasn't a gym guy. I'd done the whole membership thing, but I don't like treadmills or stationary bikes. Being a weight lifter and being sore every single day sucks. *No pain, no gain* is for the birds. I subscribe to *No pain, no problem!* Plus, getting to the gym all the time sucks. Working out in public sucks. I hated that part. I was not a fan of any of that stuff. I tried to work out on my own, in total denial that I needed that extra motivating factor.

I didn't want to be pulled into a lifestyle that was always hit-and-miss with me. I didn't love having to work out for the sake of working out. I had to be active in a way that was not going to feel like a chore and would feel like something that I was happy about doing. I wish it were enough for me to see myself in the mirror and that's your payoff. I was never big on looking in the mirror at myself. I'd rather go at my own pace and feel my clothes loosening up. And then I'd know I was living better than I used to be.

The global pandemic was a nightmare, but for me, there was one silver lining. I was super active during COVID, because there was nothing for me to do every day. I got up, made sure the girls had eaten, and went on a long bike ride. I saw crazy good results, especially when I was riding four or five times a week with my buddy Mike Piper. I thank Piper for keeping me motivated without pressuring me! At the end of each of my rides, I curled my bike like a barbell thirty times. I also did some push-ups and sit-ups. Your body's gonna react to that.

Riding my bike was my gateway to eventually loving exercise. I felt the gains, mentally and physically, immediately. Living in Manhattan, I rode my bike everywhere, winding my way through the West Village, next to the Hudson River, through Battery Park, over the Brooklyn Bridge. You really gotta know where you're going, because the farther you go, you know, the farther it is for you to ride back. Riding became totally addicting: I understand why people get sucked into bike culture and buy all the gear and wear funny little hats and shorts to decrease wind resistance. I was happy with my simple mountain bike and T-shirts and shorts. It was such a high riding my bike. After a few months of training, I could ride from Battery Park to the George Washington Bridge, and take scenic detours through Central Park and Harlem, without breaking a sweat. *Holy moly*, I'd think, smiling like a crazy person, *I didn't know I was capable of doing something so awesome!*

No, for real, it really was magical. I felt like *Tootsie* . . . without the girdle. I didn't need a girdle anymore! The physical change in me was unmistakable. Suddenly, it felt good to be able to shop at the mall. It used to feel crappy to have to sneak into the big and tall annex across the street. It was a pleasure to take a flight of stairs without huffing and puffing. When the wardrobe folks at *SNL* saw that I was losing weight, they applauded and said, "I'm so happy for you. You're loving on yourself." It felt so genuine. They had no skin in the game, they didn't have any stake in telling me I looked better or not. It was all out of love, and that really rang a bell to me. Some people think it's rude to compliment a person who has lost weight, and I do understand that, because it can insinuate you looked like an ogre before. I don't subscribe to that. The compliments I got were deeply appreciated and motivated me even more. Shout-out to Dale and Eric and Dale's sister, Donna, who runs the host around, and Tom from *SNL* wardrobe.

Throughout this journey, I've always been aware I was male privileged in the fact that I was able to work through my body awkwardness in the public eye without too much public jawing. Doesn't mean it doesn't happen to guys. Other famous actors who have struggled with their weight all their lives and have admitted that they didn't go shirtless in a pool until they were in their thirties have pleaded with their fans not to comment on their bodies.

For guys, it obviously isn't anywhere near as bad as it is for women with all the talent in the world. Forget about it. Lord knows the pressure is intense, it's mean, it's highly unfair. There's a lot of pushback against female stars who are not super thin. Look at Lizzo. I'm sure there have been plenty of heavier-set ladies who are insanely talented but never got a chance because they're in a visual medium or whatever type of excuse.

After I had baby girls, I thought about this inequity a lot. They will be bombarded with negative body image BS from now up until the rest of their lives, and I want them to be prepared. Right now, they're young enough that they haven't brought up stuff about their bodies to me. But it's coming, and *I* want to be prepared. Like Lorne, I'm going to try my darndest to model good behavior for my daughters. They are already so much more food-conscious than I ever was—they love their chicken nuggets and fries, but they will also eat red peppers and hummus, too. I'm so grateful to their mom for how they eat healthy. I always let them know there are always choices out there that are better for them. I try to turn them on to fish and vegetables and not make a stink face when I order it for myself. It's a different approach to the decision-making around eating. You make a conscious decision to choose good things to put in your body and not just throw your hands up and resort to eating garbage because it's faster or easier. Try to make healthy eating one of the natural responsibilities of life, like getting the oil changed in your car or voting.

Treating their bodies with respect should be a priority. I don't want to harp on it, because that's not good or productive, either. I've always tried to be better than what people perceive with their eyes, and I try to impart that idea to my girls. If I do a performance that's memorable, that's what people should remember first. Not my appearance. I just try to instill that they are beautiful no matter what. Feel good about yourself, independent of other people's perceptions. It doesn't matter what they say or think or do. It matters what you do.

I worry about those days when they start questioning and especially comparing themselves to others. I've heard from a lot of parents that's a really tough area. I do think you have to let them go through that journey and discover things on their own. Just keep reminding them to love themselves first. Things have changed for the better since my younger days, and I'm relieved about that. There's way more awareness around body image, eating disorders, nutrition, and having high self-esteem no matter what size you are. Lizzo is out there representing body positivity, and I admire that and adore her. But at the same time, if you're eating like an animal and never working out, that sends the wrong message as well. Loving yourself and body positivity is one thing, but it's dangerous to mix body acceptance with a disregard for health.

At the same time, fat-shaming and bullying is frowned upon a lot more than in my generation, and it's about time. You can't call someone "Chubs" in school or on social media today without, at a minimum, the fear of getting canceled. Doesn't mean it doesn't happen; surely it does. But it's not socially acceptable or PC, the phrase we used back in my day, which turned into "woke" but then was usurped by angry white people to make fun of "libtards." Unless you're Donald Trump, who calls everyone fat and ugly and gets away with it, even though he looks like that terrifying, ugly close-up picture of an ant's face.

I don't ever want to look like that ant, so keeping my dad bod in check is a priority. The message I want to impart is about the yin and yang, the balance, of life. Try to live as many years as you possibly can. You can't do that without eating right, working out your muscles, and being active on a daily basis. I used to hide my body behind a size 3X shirt that I could make hang straight. Today, I wear an XL, and I'll even tuck it in if you ask nicely. I'm five years into cutting soda, I ride my bike everywhere, and if I can bust out twenty push-ups every day, I'm good. And still very, very huggable.

······

NINE

I'm Glad I Went Broke. For Real.

Taping *Saturday Night Live* and the *Good Burger* sequel is tough on the family life, you know what I'm saying? Don't @ me—I understand that's a first-world problem, but I love my girls to pieces and want to be around them 24/7. I can't wait to get home to them at the end of the day. But all of our schedules can get pretty hectic, and quality time with my babies can be as rare as a Kobe eighty-one-point game. That's why, as often as possible, we try to have dinner together in our New York City apartment. We put down the technology, turn off whatever sporting event I have on the TV, sit at the dining room table, and have tiny child conversations.

"Daddy," Georgia will say as she pecks at her tiny food, cut up in tiny pieces on a tiny, colorful plastic plate, "a boy kicked me on the playground."

"I'm sure it was an accident," I answer.

"He was chasing me."

"Did you want him to chase you?"

She takes a sip of juice out of her tiny plastic cup. Yep, she wanted him to chase her.

"I told him not to do it anymore."

"That's good, sweetheart, you have to stand up for yourself, but still be nice. We don't put our hands on people."

When you become a dad, and your kids are in those single digits, you realize it's your job to hand out life lessons like candy. You're basically setting the dials on their moral compass for eternity. It's a lot of pressure! It's not as simple as just saying, "Do this! Don't do that!" If they say or ask something, you get about a millimeter of a second to think about it and blurt out a somewhat intelligent, profound answer. It's too easy to mess it up. You just hope and pray you're making sense and being consistent and getting through, and that in fifteen years, they won't end up prancing around in their undies on an OnlyFans account.

Parenting advice is not an exact science; still, your kids count on you to be right about everything 24/7. At first, I strived for perfection, but through trial and error, I soon realized that's an unattainable goal. Mistakes will happen; it's inevitable. The good news is, sometimes the best things in life come from questionable advice or bad decisions made by your parents. That's what happened to me.

I'm gonna tell a story now that I will tell my girls one day when they're ready to hear it, because it's chock-full of life lessons. This one kills like five birds with one stone, plus, it's such a doozy, I'm hoping any blunders I make in the future will pale in comparison.

It goes a little something like this:

By the time I was twenty-one, I had made a boatload of money starring in *All That* and *Kenan & Kel*. I'd worked really hard my whole childhood and saved every penny up to that point. I didn't really have a choice about that. I was a minor for most of those years and didn't have control over my own finances. My mom, bless her heart, hired a tax guy from the 'hood who went to her church. He had me sign a generic power-of-attorney agreement form that my mom and I bought from the office supply aisle at Walgreens. I remember thinking law shouldn't be in drugstores!

I never was allowed to go baller out of control. I never had a garage full of Bugattis like Bieber or a Bentley, a Rolls, a Ferrari, and a Lambo parked in my driveway like Kylie Jenner. This dude gave me an ATM card with a limit of $150 per day. I remember when I turned sixteen, I wanted a car and he was like, "Here's a piece-of-crap Oldsmobile Beretta!" To give you an idea of how crappy, the last Beretta rolled off the assembly line in 1996 and would be worth about $107 today. It was the featured automobile in *Coyote Ugly*, so at least there was that. But at the time, I looked at the Beretta and said, "No thanks, I definitely don't want that."

Kel and I had a good run as the "Kings of Nickelodeon," but all good things come to an end. We weren't Peter Pan. We grew up, as people do, and it was time to be pushed out of the nest. Problem was, when the kids' comedy gravy train ended, I was a little lost.

I was living in LA but wasn't working much. My baby face has always been a blessing and a curse. I was already famous but too young-looking to get adult roles. My managers sent my tapes to *Saturday Night Live* casting directors multiple times, but I kept getting rejected for looking too young. It felt like a made-up excuse. Eddie managed to get on when he was only nineteen. My son Pete Davidson got on when he was twenty. I'm no Eddie Murphy or Pete Davidson, but they didn't have ten years of experience under their belts or multiple sketch shows of their own like I did.

I couldn't figure out where in Hollywood I fit in, so I started hanging out at the Black comedy nights at the stand-up clubs around town, thinking that might be my new jam. Chocolate Sundaes at the Laugh Factory, Monday nights at the Improv, Fat Tuesdays at the Comedy Store. I was obsessed with comedy, and I loved that world. I caught pop-ins of legendary comics like George Wallace and Martin Lawrence, plus the early years of geniuses like Mike Epps, when they were just crushing it onstage and hadn't been discovered yet.

As much as I loved being there, I wasn't welcomed with open arms by most of the up-and-comers. In their eyes, I was already rich and famous; I could afford a two-drink minimum but was wasting it on ginger ales, and they were struggling to break in and made $100 per night, tops. They didn't want me there. They didn't want me to steal their time, their mojo, or their jokes. I was like, *I'm not here to do any of that! I'm just here because I can drink strawberry daiquiris here.* I didn't want to step on toes and make anyone feel a type of way, so I stopped going, which truly broke my heart. If I knew back then what I knew now, I'd say eff them and their two-drink minimum. But at the time, it hurt.

Brian Robbins was one of the head honchos at *All That* and helped me land on my feet when I moved to Los Angeles. He was my second dad, a true mentor. The first true "Hollywood" memory I can remember was driving his car during my first visit to LA. No Lambo or anything too shiny, just a high-end Land Cruiser, which might as well have been a Lambo to me. Even in front-to-butt traffic straight out of a "Californians" sketch, I felt like I was sitting on a chrome throne, high above the peasants in sedans.

One night I was driving down Wilshire to the beach at night, sunroof open, soaking in the summer LA weather best described as "nonexistent." In the pre-smartphone era, red lights were an opportunity to smile at anyone who dared to look over at the Black man in the big truck. For the first time, ambition took over, and I thought, *Oh man, I want this to be a part of my life. If this is the game, I want to be a player in it.*

With my Nickelodeon contract officially ending January 1, 2000, I was sort of paralyzed and needed space to figure out my next move, so I decided to get out of Dodge and go home to my mom's house in Atlanta for the holidays. I was confused about my future but also scared the world might end because of Y2K. If we were all gonna die,

I was gonna do it surrounded by my family and my closest childhood friends. So we threw a house party on New Year's Eve. At the stroke of midnight, everybody was still dancing and not really paying attention to the fact that all the lights were still on, and no planes fell out of the sky and crashed on our heads.

"Yo!" I called out merrily. "Everything is fine! The missiles didn't launch! We're not blowing up! None of that type of stuff is happening!"

The party guests let out a hearty "Heyyyyyyy!" but I can't lie, I had a short beat where I froze in terror, thinking, *Um, if life indeed is going to continue, I'm gonna have to figure out what the heck I'm gonna do with my future. SWAT training? Nah.* I snapped out of my trance, shoved the scary adulting stuff into the back of my mind, and went straight back to doing the Running Man to "My Boo" with everybody else (I would explain to my girls that was the equivalent to a TikTok dance today).

For the next few months, I pushed those thoughts as far back in my brain as a COVID test cotton Q-tip. I had money in the bank and deserved a little break, I convinced myself. I got real comfy—too comfy—hanging at my mom's house, sleeping on the bunk beds in my old room surrounded by all of the memorabilia I'd collected in my career so far: a hockey stick from *D2: The Mighty Ducks*, a framed pair of boxers Da Brat signed after guesting on an episode of *All That* (I think they were my boxers. I didn't have anything else for her to sign!), and a signed autograph by Jim Carrey, gifted to me by Judd Apatow.

Every day, instead of thinking about going back to work, I hung out with my childhood buddies in one of our basements.

Back in those days, we were all about having a good time. So, you know, it was raging hormones and turning the music on and let's see who can do the most bumping and grinding without any conflict (earmuffs, my pets). We might not have been the popular jocks or those rascals in the chess club, but we theater geeks still knew how to party. Every night my boys and I hung out in the streets and went clubbing all over Atlanta. I was medium famous, but nobody treated me any different. Amongst people my age, I wasn't that big of a deal. Unless someone had kids, nobody was really tripping on me being in the same club as them. Maybe Steve from *Blue's Clues* got his clothes torn off, but not this fella.

My mom was happy I was there, and my old friends liked having me around. That was the best part because I was just chilling back home with them. We could still have a good time just being in someone's basement playing video games. Everything was fine! Until it wasn't.

In my opinion, I was a rich man in Atlanta, and I wasn't feeling super ambitious. One day, after very little thought, I proclaimed, "I think I'm going to buy a house around here!" A starter home in my neighborhood would only cost about four hundred grand, and in my mind, I figured, *Well, I got that in my sleep!*

I'd only looked at a couple places when, *bingo was his name-o,* I found my ultimate dream home. Drumroll, please . . . This house had two staircases, *just like on The Cosby Show.* Are you kidding? I almost wept when I saw it. There was one staircase in the foyer and a spiral one that came down from the master bedroom into the kitchen. Oh my God, it was incredible. It looked like something I'd seen on *Lifestyles of the Rich and Famous*, which today would be *Cribs*! I thought to myself, *Well, good sir, this might as well be Beverly Hills!*

It wasn't. It was Southwest Atlanta. But I saw those two staircases, pictured myself descending them in a colorful knit Coogi sweater after a sexy night with a ladyfriend, and I was done, man. Plus, it was literally around the corner from my mom's house. We could borrow cups of sugar from each other anytime we wanted, day or night, in our pajamas. I saw it as a sign from God, or Cosby himself—at the time, one of my biggest comedic heroes. I'll get into that devolution more in depth later, promise.

I made an offer immediately, at full asking price. Never do that, Georgia Marie and Gianna Michelle, you hear me?

I did that. In my opinion, at that moment, I felt like once I owned my own house, I was pretty much set for life. No stress ever again because I knew where I was going to lay my head every night. My new house with *not one, but two* staircases was my future, my foundation. I was good. I could act more or not. You know what I'm saying?

I was literally about to retire at the age of twenty-one, when the gods of humility got their sweet vengeance, and it all came crashing down on me like a sledgehammer. Remember my accountant, Mr. Beretta? In the beginning, he started out protecting me from being too wild with my money then, when I wasn't paying attention, mostly because I was just a kid and didn't know what I was supposed to be paying attention to. There'd been red flags everywhere all along, but they were well disguised as keeping me penny-wise.

Five years on from the great Beretta incident, here I was, making the first, the biggest, the realest financial decision of my adult life—buying myself a house. Suddenly, and not at all surprisingly, my trusty accountant went MIA, or ghosted me, as the kids say today. When he failed to show up at the meeting to do escrow and sign all that real estatey stuff, I got that kick-in-the-gut, heart-sinking kinda feeling. As I sat in front of the lawyers and brokers all by myself, looking like a shady, broke-ass fool, my face burned up in humiliation. I knew I'd been conned.

I called my accountant a million times, and when he didn't answer my fifty-seventh message pleading with him to get back to me ASAP, I decided to take matters into my own hands. Atlanta back then was like a small town, especially my neighborhood. I knew exactly where the dude lived.

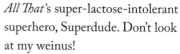

All That's super-lactose-intolerant superhero, Superdude. Don't look at my weinus!

(Tollin/Robbins Productions / Courtesy of Everett Collection)

I love calling us the "Original Seven."

(Nickelodeon / Courtesy of Everett Collection)

I look very, very young but I was full-on fifteen years old in this picture!

(Moviestore Collection Ltd / Alamy Stock Photo)

Two oldies named Mavis and Clavis and a baby Usher

Just three rookies hanging in the mirror. Kobe Bryant was the homie: Mamba for life!

Good Burger, great pic. This is definitely one of my favorite photos of Kel and me. We were just two wide-eyed, happy kids living the dream.

(*AJ Pics / Alamy Stock Photo / © PARAMOUNT*)

Sticking a long probe down my throat to fix the vocal cord polyps I got while going through puberty. Everybody should try it once.

Early '80s Thompsons. Clues: my mom is holding a Tab and my brother has an Asteroids shirt on.

Which one of us didn't pay taxes and which one is Wesley Snipes?

Early Arsenio Hall inspiration coming through. Tryin' to look good for the lay-days!

Left: I was a running back in peewee football. I wish I still had this old-school Houston Oilers helmet!

Below: Quietly giving thanks in the back of a weird white line. I'm the same age as those dudes, but notice the height. By the way, we did take this play about Christopher Columbus to Spain, his homeland dontcha know!

Cutie in a tank top!

Cutie in a bow tie!

A *Mighty Ducks* mini-reunion

It's knuckle puck time!

They told us to look "*GQ* sexy" for the *Heavyweights* promo shot. This is what we came up with.

(AJ Pics / Alamy Stock Photo / Disney)

Pete Davidson stopped by to support me before I hosted the 2022 Emmys. My little brother Pete. Family forever. Good guy.

Trying not to shart my pants during the opening performance at the Emmys

(Mark Terrill)

I had just told Lorne a joke that was much funnier to me. Thank you for everything, Lorne.

There's a blanket of comfort that some people bring to your life. Bowen Yang is that.

Siblings on vacay!

Have you ever been on a real live stakeout?

I have. One time.

At eleven p.m., my buddy and I jumped into my car. It was no Beretta, but it had four wheels and an engine. For dramatic effect I'd like to say my buddy jumped through the window, and I slid across the hood like Bo and Luke in *The Dukes of Hazzard*, but that would be a bald-faced lie. We just opened the doors, got in normally, drove over to his house, minding the speed limit, and parked in his driveway.

We sat in front of his house all night, waiting for a light to turn on, looking for any sign of movement. Our overnight surveillance was not like what you see in a Hollywood movie. Nobody ordered us delivery take-out pizza like my hero Eddie Murphy did as Axel Foley in *Beverly Hills Cop*. There was no witty banter between us like Richard Dreyfuss and Emilio Estevez in *Stakeout*, and there was definitely no romance. Not that there's anything wrong with that.

My buddy and I talked for six hours straight, but I couldn't tell you about what—I was too rattled. I had no concept of time. I didn't eat, and I don't even think I had to pee. Eating and peeing seems . . . *unimportant*, shall we say . . . when your entire life savings has been stolen from you.

It also didn't occur to me that what we were doing was kind of dangerous. Homie had a big German shepherd behind his gate, and I vaguely recall plotting out our insurrection and directing, "Okay, we're taking the dog down first!" That's just awful. Who had I become? This was not me. Kenan S. Thompson was more lover than fighter.

Like I taught my girls, I'm not the kicker-on-the-playground type. I do not condone violence, nor do I instigate it. Usually. Usually. There was that one time I accidentally wore a full-on matching San Francisco Giants outfit, including a nice black-and-orange jacket, to an LA Dodgers game, and they weren't even playing the Giants. Only people who have a death wish or work for a South American cartel can get away with wearing SF merch to a Dodgers game. It was about to get serious. Luckily, this kid who was dressed as Nacho Libre recognized me from *All That*, and everybody stopped pelting me with peanuts and bought me beers the rest of the night. Everyone forgave me, so it was a good time.

This particular stakeout was not a good time. Finally, at six a.m., my cell phone rang. It was my accountant. He wasn't happy. *Excuse me, I believe I get to be the unhappy one here?* "My neighbors told me there's been a car parked in my driveway all night," he whined. "That you?"

"Yeah, that's me," I answered, not as intimidating as I'd hoped. "You need to talk to me. What's up?" I think my voice cracked on "up." I was still just a youngin, know what I mean?

He made a bunch of lame excuses and told me to meet him at the bank when it opened. I raced over as soon as the doors unlocked, and to my amazement, he was there, too. I let him do that dance of, "My bad, I'll fix it, I'll fix it," naïvely holding out hope everything was legit and gonna be all right. He went inside to fetch my house money, but after I stood outside like a scrub for an hour, the "fix" was officially in.

I never saw him, or my million dollars, ever again.

Around the same time, the IRS also came after me because the dude never paid any of my taxes. I was broke and couldn't pay off any of my penalty, and believe me when I say it was a large chunk. So I was forced into bankruptcy. It was pretty gnarly. And it affected me for years after. Meanwhile, thanks to our justice system and tax loopholes, my crooked accountant never went to jail. Sure, I eventually sued and won, but it didn't matter. The money was gone. I hope he at least paid for a new kidney or put his kids through college on my dime.

I wasn't supposed to be broke and bankrupt. I mean, I was Pierre Escargot. Dexter from *Good Burger*. The knuckle puck master from *The Mighty Ducks*, for the love of Russ! This was not how my life was supposed to go. My poor mom took full responsibility and the blame and, to this day, feels absolutely awful and guilty and mortified about hiring the accountant. But whenever she gets down about it, I always squeeze her tight and remind her that I never really had access to my own money in the first place, so I didn't really miss it when it was gone.

Luckily, I had very good, kind people around me who kept reminding me that my financial troubles were not the end of the world. I remember hanging out in my buddy's kitchen in Atlanta one night and having one of those life-changing epiphanies usually reserved for teary guests on Oprah's *Super Soul Sunday*. "I think I'm going to have to just move back to LA and get it back cracking," I suddenly announced. Retirement was over. That was a huge moment.

You may be thinking, *Good Lord, Kenan Thompson, you have such an inspiring attitude!* Listen, when we were sitting in my accountant's driveway, I had visions of punching the gas and driving my car through the front window of his house like a Blues Brother, but fortunately (or unfortunately), that's just not me. And in this situation, I didn't feel like I had another choice than to take the L like a man and move on. It was hopeless to be upset because I didn't have control. If I let this dude cripple or sideline me, then I was defeating my own purpose. That would have been the greater tragedy.

My philosophy became, *Let me just get back to work and chalk it up to the game. Whatever will come, will come.* My mantra became, *That's his karma, not my karma.*

I'm not downplaying my bankruptcy, it was devastating, but it actually kicked my butt into gear. I was this close to being a single, sleazebag kind of guy who lazed about for the rest of his life, but I can't lie, I would've been good with the double staircase, know what I mean? All of a sudden, I had purpose and drive again. I *knew* I was good at performing comedy. The one thing I knew I could literally do the next day was to head back to LA and get back into the rhythm of auditioning and working. Then I could pay off my debt. I was willing to take any job, whether I played a hot dog vendor or had a starring role, as long as it led to the next gig.

A lesson I learned the hard way: filing for bankruptcy changes a man's life. For too many years during this period, I had no credit; I was forced to move every summer, and couldn't rent my own apartment unless I paid an entire year in advance. I was so embarrassed about it for the longest time. I had to call a couple of my buddies every now and again to borrow a hundred bucks here, a couple hundred bucks there, just to get through the day.

My mom, God bless her, was a nurse, so she could only lend me a hundred bucks every now and again. Thank God this wasn't the age of social media, because today, everybody knows all your business. Outside of a few close friends and family members, I never told anyone my deepest, most humbling secret.

Twenty years later, I'm still traumatized about what happened. It showed me real hardship outside of my comfort zone. I didn't have any kind of safety net, because I didn't have a bunch of rich friends. I had to just dive back into trying to get back into the game as an adult. I already had a work drive, but having everything taken away kicked my butt into overdrive.

Another good thing my situation taught me early on, the hard way, was what money did to people and how people use it to manipulate other people. I'm thankful that I was never that dude who blew his fortune and ended up in a Netflix documentary twenty years later, missing an arm after an alligator attack. Hang on, that was *Tiger King*.

There are several morals to my bankruptcy story: it's about humility for sure, and also not taking anything for granted because it can all be gone tomorrow. It's also about cutting your parents some slack—they did/they're doing the best they can. I love my mom to pieces; she is an absolute angel, and while it's true that one single decision she made led to the worst thing to ever happen in my life, I learned that everything happens for a reason.

My bankruptcy was horrible and affected my life for years, but there was a huge silver lining: If I didn't go broke, neither of the two best things in my life—being on *SNL* and having my beautiful girls—would have happened.

I'm still looking for a house with two staircases, though. Let me know if you have any leads. Thanks, I appreciate you.

TEN

······

There's a Thin Line Between Perseverance and Delusion

B ack in the late '90s, I was partying in a club when, lo and behold, Justin Timberlake and Britney Spears walked in, hand in hand. I knew them in a casual way, as we were all in the same orbit of child stardom. Britney and Justin were a brand-new, bold-faced pairing. Justin's curly blond 'fro was fresh, and their conscious coupling was still very new. The two hit the dance floor, and Britney was just *killing it*. Justin was trying to keep up—no doubt, the kid could dance his skinny butt off, too—but it was like watching a boy try to hold on to a bronco. She was throwing hair and hips and this, that, and the other. It was crazy. JT couldn't hold a candle to a young Britney Spears in her prime. As I watched this iconic spectacle, sipping on gin and juice, I had an epiphany. *Sir Kenan Thompson*, I thought to myself, *you're in the right place.* Because if Britney and Justin were here and I was here, too, that meant I'd made it. I was floating amongst the rich and famous in the TMZ, the thirty-mile zone of Hollywood.

What I didn't realize at the time was that life can change on a dime and it could be over faster than a blond curly 'fro on a white boy. I distinctly remember the moment when my career cratered. When I was about twenty-one, right after I "graduated" from Nickelodeon, I was a guest on *The Tonight Show with Jay Leno*. During the pre-interview, I boasted to the producers that I could do a spot-on impersonation of Jay. That was a lie. I'd never really worked on it. I did an impression of him that was lazy, unpolished, and borderline insulting—just his high voice and a lisp. I don't even remember what I said; I've locked it in a vault in my brain somewhere. You could hear a pin drop, then Jay finally said, "I don't think that sounds like me at all." That bit ended up on the cutting room floor, and I was never asked back to the show again. Like ever. Which to this day just crushes and embarrasses me. Sorry, Jay. I was young and dumb.

It got worse from there. After my money was stolen and I moved back to LA, there were some really hard times. I wasn't impoverished, but it was the kind of struggle where you let your brakes squeak to save a few bucks. Like, when you pull up to a stop sign, and all the dogs in the neighborhood start howling. All of a sudden, I was a barely legal kid from the other side of the country with no job and no prospects.

This was the beginning of a three-year gap of weirdness in my life where I had a loooooot of free time on my hands.

I knew I had to get back to work and back to supporting myself. LA was the only place I knew where I could just fall out of the house and wind up on *The $20,000 Pyramid* game show as a celebrity contestant or some other easy hustle, just by being local and a recognizable name in some circles. I remember going to my buddy Tac's place in Atlanta and sitting in his kitchen venting to him all day and all night for two straight days, processing my situation. "I gotta go back to LA. I gotta do it," I kept saying. He agreed it was the right thing to do. I guess I needed validation from someone who knew me well. I was so grateful Tac let me bend his ear and he had my back.

Josh, my best friend from *All That*, was still in the Hollywood hustle, and he encouraged me to come back to LA and get back in that hustle mode. So I went back to LA, rented a car, and Josh was kind enough to let me crash on his couch until I was on my feet again. Josh helped me tap into my artistic side again. We tentpoled each other. We ran lines together for auditions, and watched artsy indie movies like *The Basketball Diaries* together to dissect the actors' performances. Josh and I were so close, and he was one of the only people I ever told about my money being stolen. He knew, when I left Atlanta for LA, that I only had enough cash left to sideways hustle.

I wasn't so far removed from working, so I was still in the habit of picking up the phone, calling my agent and manager, and seeing what was cracking as well. But when you're in between solid jobs, interest in you dies down, and you get tired of asking over and over, "Does anybody need a face for the Long Beach Dog Show?" I envied my former *All That* castmates, like Angelique and Katrina, who were doing signings at Comic-Con and smaller events around the country. I was more, "Any famous athletes need a face for their celebrity weekend golf tournament?" (Those paid like ten grand; let me get one of those.) I tried to be out on the scene enough to be aware of whoever might be doing such a thing, but then it got exhausting and depressing because those things have nothing to do with your craft. You're chasing a hundred bucks here, a thousand bucks there. And it hit me: *What am I really doing?*

I kicked my auditioning hustle into full gear and tried to book what I could. I went back and forth with my manager a million times. Shout-out to Michael Goldman, because he was right there with me the whole time. He's been my one and only manager and a good dude. Agents come and go, but Michael has remained a constant. He doesn't pull punches; he's one person in my life that never sugarcoats anything and doesn't blow smoke up my butt. I will say that one silver lining of being robbed of my life savings was it made me get better at reading people and their intentions, earlier than later. Working with Michael was one of the best decisions I've ever made.

I started going on auditions, but I had some stiff competition. I was always up against Anthony Anderson, future star of *Black-ish*. I'd show up and see his name on the call sheet and know he'd just left. Anthony is my brother to this day. He has the most infectious laugh of anyone I've ever met. Like me, he just wanted to make everybody laugh and have a good time. And that's how we connected. The first time I met him, he tackled me into a wall, and made me laugh so hard I farted. He's one of my favorite people in the world.

While I often encountered Anthony and other comedians like Mike Epps during auditions, I was never like, *Eff them, this is* my *role, this is* my *chance*. I believed that there was room for all of us to succeed. And we had different goals. None of us was trying to be the Ryan Gosling or Robert Pattinson of the time. It was different for Black people. What I wanted to be was a Morris Chestnut, one of those steady character actors booking roles. At that point, it seemed like being an Eddie Murphy was such a conundrum because fame was taking a toll; it didn't seem like even he wanted to deal with it anymore. People like Anthony and Mike and I, we had our own world, and, in my opinion, our world was entertaining our grandparents. Like if Grandma ain't happy, then you ain't doin' shit. I let the idea of Eddie Murphy–level fame go.

During this period in my life, I auditioned for so many projects that I forgot that I'd auditioned for some of them. And then I'd see a movie and recognize the dialogue. *Oh snap, I remember these words*, I'd think. *I guess I didn't book that one*. I focused so hard on the actor hustle, the *let me go to a convention in Arizona really quick and sign some* All That *merch* vibe started tapering off. I was giving 110 percent to making sure I could subsidize my life with acting gigs. I traded in my rental car and bought myself a brand-new Toyota 4Runner, the first

SUV to get really popular after Ford Broncos became taboo thanks to OJ Simpson's getaway—I mean, joyride. My truck was the first big purchase I'd ever made in my life. Wasn't a Cosby house with a spiral staircase, but it was my pride and joy. It was black with gold stripes, had a sick sound system, and the back window rolled down, halfway or all the way, driver's choice. I was flying around the streets of greater Los Angeles in my 4Runner, flipping through my giant Thomas Guide to find my auditions.

I convinced Josh, who now had a side hustle in real estate, that we should move into a house right behind a Fatburger in the San Fernando Valley. We partied all the time, and, unfortunately, we lived right next to the landlord, and he did not opt to renew our lease. I found us a new house up the hill from Jerry's Deli, the one that had a bowling alley in it on Ventura. I bought a bedroom set from IKEA. I had no eye for decor. I just knew I could get a bed, dresser, and nightstand that matched, and I said, "Sign me up." The 4Runner and my light beige bedroom furniture were all I technically owned. Josh and I rented out the third bedroom to cut costs, and that revolving roommate became our very own Spinal Tap drummer. It was a revolving door of kooky characters who, by the way, rarely paid their rent. One guy seemed so cool, quiet, and humble. He said he had plenty of cash and his dog was chill. "We won't bother anybody." His dog was not chill. It was a giant Doberman that swallowed up every room it was in and terrorized people. It was the dog from hell. And, of course, the guy disappeared and had a million excuses on the first of every month.

I could always depend on Josh to be on time with his money and be responsible. _I_ was struggling. After I booked anything, I hounded my agents and lawyers to get paid. It was humbling. "I need the money," I'd say sheepishly.

At least I was struggling around people I thoroughly enjoyed the company of and in a place I loved. I was always highly infatuated with

LA. I loved California life—the weather, the women, all of it. I was still young, and I had a brand-new crib. I had enough cash to throw baller barbecues with beer can chicken and sausages and medium-shelf liquor. Because Josh and I were two young guys with no boundaries, we had an open-door policy at our residences. We let just about anybody come hang out, eat all our food, drink all our alcohol, and stay as long as they wanted. We had friends who were dancers on *Soul Train* (shout-out to Curt Boogie) and, after they taped on Saturdays, rolled over to our place for the after-party. One of the dancers became a talent booker and started bringing all sorts of random people over. Those hangouts turned into all-nighters, and the next morning, when everyone opened their bleary eyes, the conversation became, "What are you up to today?" Then collectively as a group we'd all go and do that thing.

I didn't know how to hustle up money from nowhere, but they did. I started going on what I affectionately refer to as my "California adventures." I'd drop people off at their homes and hang out with them in their environment, maybe meet their auntie in Pasadena or their cousin in Van Nuys. Who knew, we might come upon some good times for free. Let's just go see.

I'm not gonna lie, I was mostly hanging out with not the greatest people. Not necessarily bad people. You know, the type who knew how to hustle up $100 a day and had four degrees of separation from Snoop Dogg, so we'd end up at Snoop Dogg's house. True story. This one guy who stayed at my Fatburger house for only God knows how long was a singer. He said he was down with Snoop and was gonna sing on his next record. I had my doubts because he'd been wedged into my couch for a minute, hadn't once offered to buy toilet paper, and I'd never once even heard him sing a few notes in the shower, but what did I know? Anyway, this dude was street level, somewhat in the Snoop gang; he even rolled up his sleeve and showed me a Dogg Pound tattoo.

Well, apparently, I knew nothing, because we ended up at Snoop's house and Snoop knew him by name. So I was like, *Well, I was wrong, and I guess we can kick it.* And we kicked it at Snoop's studio house all day, watched him make records, hung out with his brother, and smoked so much wacky tobaccy, we were basically baked beans. At a point, Snoop was like, "All right, I'm going to bed," and I couldn't believe we'd outsmoked Snoop Dogg, the undisputed GOAT of ganja.

I didn't make any kind of connection with Snoop or any future plans to do business, but flash forward to years later, when I was on *SNL*, and we bumped into each other in a club.

"Hey, man," he said, all friendly. "You remember my guy Tippy Toes?" Snoop was referring to my unassuming houseguest who'd brought us to his house long ago.

"Tippy Toes" was not ol' boy's name, by the way. I made that up on a rap name generator to protect the innocent. Who could forget Tippy Toes? Or the night I spent in Snoop's studio? One of the greatest moments of my life. By this point, I'd been around plenty of famous people, but meeting Snoop was very cool for me. He'd probably had thousands of people around him in his lifetime, but he remembered the night we first met, too. I was such a fan, so it was very special. And PS—to anyone who says weed rots your brain, Snoop's memory was as crystal clear as a glass water pipe.

That time in my life was a tipping point. You know, forks in the road and all that. If things were gonna go south in a textbook-tragic child-star way, that would have been it. My career was at a standstill, I didn't have a lot of money, and I was rolling with some questionable acquaintances. It was a very vulnerable place to be. Not to say I didn't have it in me to go down a dark road. I think everybody does. I just didn't want to do that. Bottom line is that I always had faith that one day things would turn over. If they didn't, I'd go drive a bus. I knew I'd be okay either way.

I did almost quit acting and came really close to throwing in the towel. I'm glad I didn't. For all you young'uns out there, the fledgling actors who don't know if they should keep pressing or head back to Gary, Indiana, it's like Kenny Rogers once said, "You gotta know when to hold 'em, know when to fold 'em." There's a fine line between perseverance and being delusional, but I do think my little bit of denial of my situation and my naïveté are what saved me. I wasn't really admitting to myself that I'd hit rock bottom. I'd tell myself every day to just keep hustling; I knew I'd figure things out, that I'd figure out how to be a working actor. Thankfully, I never once filed for unemployment to get help. That was my sign to myself that I should keep pressing. Also, you had to stand in line for a really long time back then for unemployment benefits, and spending a day doing paperwork just wasn't in my spirit.

I think having the Spinal Tap roommates gave me a little bit of perspective. They were struggling to come up with one room's worth of rent. In my mind, I had the bigger responsibility kind of mindset and was able to handle that. I knew I should be able to eventually get to a point where I could handle it all on my own, as opposed to noticing they were lost in the fog, not really knowing what they wanted to do professionally. They didn't have a track record in any one specific direction; they dabbled in music or modeling but nothing that was bona fide. I was coming off having two television shows as a kid and trying to figure out how to transfer that into an adult career. I felt like I was going to figure it out eventually. One of these days it'll be all right.

In the meantime, I always had Steve Harvey's mantra in my brain, going over and over: *Say yes to everything.* And then, like a miracle, from Steve's lips to God's ear, I booked a role on the *Untitled Sisqó Pilot*, starring R & B singer Sisqó and Bob Newhart. Yes, the dude who made "Thong Song" was the top bill over one of the most iconic stand-up comedians in history, and no, it never got a title. We spent a whole week shooting it, and even taped in front of a live studio audience, like it was an episode of *That's My Mama* or something, so that was awesome.

(If you're wondering, the chemistry was there between Sisqó and Bob, but I admit it was difficult to get past how weird and unnecessary this show felt. Nobody could shake it. If you Google "Untitled Sisqó Project," there's literally no plot description, and four entries down, the listing info is in Russian. I'm drawing a blank on the plot, too, but I do recall there was a porch scene with just the two of them having a heart-to-heart, and to be honest, it was super funny. Bob was incredible. I mean, he's an older guy, generically nice to everybody, but it was still like, there's one of the GOATs right there. Part of his deal was shooting it in his comfort zone. So we were in the sound stage where he'd done both *Newhart* and *The Bob Newhart Show*, which was on Bob Newhart Drive on the CBS Radford lot in Studio City. He used the same dressing room he'd had for like fourteen years. That's gangsta.)

Even though the show sounds sort of silly, it had a huge impact on me. It was my first inkling that I should hold on to a job for as long as humanly possible. Seeing that with Bob, fourteen years in the same place, same set, same dressing room, was inspirational. Stability was appealing to me. Before that, the goal was to blow up and be as famous as possible. Now, after hustling from gig to gig in my 4Runner, I could appreciate a steady job again.

I always knew one job led to another if you did it right. That was always my belief: that once you're in, people will continue to use you. It was slightly naïve, but it also gave me a fake confidence to go out there every day and do my best in a room full of strangers, especially now that I didn't necessarily have a home on TV. Each job opportunity became, *All right, I gotta show up and prove what it is that makes me special.* My mentality was to go kill it all the time.

My theory proved to be right on. The next thing I booked was a recurring guest star role on *Felicity*. *Felicity* was my first experience wearing a fat suit in a serious role. The show gave me this super-pillowy, ridiculous fat suit, so I looked super awkward, like you'd look at me and think, *What is happening with this person?* I didn't really care; I needed the job. Put me in a sumo suit, whatever, I'm there. The plot was heavy, about a character having eye surgery, and she met my character with bandages over her eyes. She fell in love with my voice, but then when she actually saw me after the bandages came off, she had to decide if she was still attracted to me. She ended up choosing to give me a chance. It had a sweet ending; her character didn't diss my character, and I didn't feel like I dissed myself climbing into the fat suit. Rather than for laughs, donning the suit felt more like a device, used to add gravitas to a serious topic. I felt maybe my portrayal had done a service for real-life people who did have that reality.

After *Felicity*, I booked a sprinkling of some voice-over gigs, then the teen movie *Love Don't Cost a Thing*, starring my old pal Nick Cannon and Christina Milian. It was one of those it's-good-to-have-friends moments. I needed a job; Nick's career was cracking, and he brought me on to the project. It was a beautiful thing.

I was just an actor for hire, sure, but I was still picky about certain things. I was chubby at the time. In this movie, there was a locker room scene where we were supposed to have our shirts off. I declined to take my shirt off. And it became *a thing*. The director didn't really appreciate my refusal; she believed I was infringing on her vision. For me, I thought it unusual to have a shower scene set in a high school. So I stuck to my guns. I was uncomfortable, and I felt like it wasn't going to be anything flattering for the movie, so why do it? The only reason I've ever taken my shirt off in a movie is because I couldn't leave my buddy Zach Levi hanging out to dry. That's the only time you've ever seen me with my shirt off.

I think the universe rewards you for good decisions that are authentic to who you are. Three years after my money was stolen, I was flown to Chicago for the summer to film *Barbershop 2*, a blockbuster franchise starring Ice Cube, my old pal Cedric the Entertainer, and the rapper Eve. I had a small but pivotal role. It was the first job in a long while that was paying me semi-decently, and I'd get a per diem, so I wouldn't have to think about money for a couple months. It was high-profile. It was Black zeitgeist.

I was a little nervous because everybody was expecting me to impress them during rehearsal. Cedric was killing everybody; they knew they could rely on him. I was more like the smell of a new car. Like, *Who's this new funny guy? Does he stink or what?* Ice Cube was a tough crowd. He wasn't the type to laugh out loud, and he spoke volumes with his reactions. If you could get him to look at you and let out a small chuckle, that was his seal of approval.

In my first scene, I come into the barbershop for the first time, and Ice Cube is hiring me. So it's like, *Bam, here I am, this is my character.* I ran with it. I was like a tornado running through the set, delivering lines, being loud, just going wild. I got that chuckle from him, and I was over the moon. Everyone knows that he pretty much is credited with discovering Chris Tucker. *Friday* could have been a gangster movie easily, but it turned out to be a comedy because Ice Cube enjoys comedy. He found Chris and was like, *Oh, I can just let this guy run.* That's also a sign of talent and genius, knowing how to find and nurture talent. By the time I got to the very last week, I was like the set mascot, being nurtured and mentored yet again by the coolest people.

Eve was at the top of her game, in the middle of being peak Eve. Instead of a honey wagon trailer, she had a full tour bus because, duh, she was a rapper. Eve was so generous with her time and money. She took all of us to the movies a bunch of times, and I got to hang with the Ruff Ryders.

I had to go through a bankruptcy and rip my life down to the grass foundation and start over. It definitely got murky after Nickelodeon. Shit got real. It was painful but an essential part of my life journey. That summer on *Barbershop 2* was life-changing—I started to feel deep in my bones that my downward spiral was trending back upward. The last week of shooting, I got a phone call from my manager. I had to fly to New York City ASAP. I finally had a shot at an audition for *Saturday Night Live*.

ELEVEN

I Want You to Be Proud of Me, Too

I don't shove the showbiz life down my kids' throats. At the same time, I'm proud of my career, and one day, when they're old enough to understand, I want them to see what it took for me to make it and for them to be proud of me, too. I love telling the inspiring, suspenseful tale of how I finally landed *SNL*, a story that means everything to me.

As I've said before, my baby face has always been a blessing and a curse. At the height of my Nickelodeon stardom, I was a poster child for the kids' network, and my face was plastered all over its airwaves 24/7. Post-Nickelodeon, my agents kept sending my reel to the casting directors of *Saturday Night Live* but kept hearing back that I looked too young. It felt like an excuse. But at the time, industry folks considered me a baby, even though I was in my twenties—I could go to war, vote, and fold fitted sheets. I was adulting, man.

I also wondered whether my constant rejection from *SNL* was because I lacked a traditional *SNL* pedigree; I'd never taken classes at renowned improv theaters like Second City in Chicago (where Tina Fey perfected her sketch comedy chops), or the Groundlings in LA (the birthplace of Maya Rudolph and so many other *SNL* stars). *All*

That had billed itself as "*SNL* for kids," but that didn't seem to be good enough training.

I'd been down in the minor leagues for so long, I wasn't sure I'd ever make it to the majors. I soon struggled to see myself standing next to the Adam Sandlers and Will Ferrells of the world. I couldn't picture myself actually being on the show because it was so iconic. I slowly started to let go of the dream and continued to pound the pavement, because my 4Runner's brakes were squealing, and I had crazy roommates who skipped out on their rent. Whatever job came my way, I'd take it to pay the bills.

That was my vibe until I booked *Barbershop 2*. Suddenly, I was rubbing shoulders with Black Hollywood A-listers again. At least I was progressing in an upward trajectory. Not that *Felicity* wasn't a cool experience—that's where I met JJ Abrams, who'd become the future prolific writer/producer/director of *Lost*, plus several *Mission: Impossible* and *Star Wars* movies. At the same time, *Felicity* was so outside of my wheelhouse, I didn't feel like I fit in, because they were three seasons deep by that point. It's not that I was mad when Keri Russell cut her hair off; it just felt like a onetime gig. Then *Love Don't Cost a Thing* was great, but that was Nick's movie, I had a sidekicky role, and it wasn't the biggest payday in the world.

After Tracy Morgan left *SNL* in 2003, I guess all of a sudden I looked old enough. I finally got the call to audition. I was like, *All right, here we go.*

Honestly, it's kind of messed up when people insinuate *You got so-and-so job because they needed a Black guy* (or an Asian woman, or a Hispanic dude, whatever flavor outside vanilla) because it discounts the talent and hard work you put in to get there. I was just one guy who had spent almost half of my life doing sketch comedy, taking advantage of the small window of opportunity presented to me. Today, there are a lot more windows for more voices, which is amazing. I can't wait 'til we get to the point where it's all windows—one big greenhouse, growing comedy plants of all shapes and sizes.

Around the same time, I had been hanging around with Whoopi Goldberg's daughter, Alex, a lot, at Whoopi's compound in LA. I met Alex through my cousin Taadow—shout-out to him because he's one person who has had my back for years. Whoopi had always been so nice to me, but her daughter was super cool. I'd go over there and watch Floyd Mayweather fights and stuff. The reason I'm dropping this tidbit is because I'll never forget what Alex said to me when I found out I got the *SNL* audition: "Go book that." Sounds simple, but she just knew. I had her voice echoing in my mind the entire time, so shout-out to Alex for putting that in the universe.

I hit the road and headed straight from the *Barbershop 2* set in Chicago right to New York City, like a hobo with a stick and a handkerchief stuffed with a couple pairs of dirty underpants. I didn't even go home first. I couldn't wait to see what was cracking in Manhattan. They put me up at the Paramount in Times Square, a hotel with a bohemian vibe, which means it was the size of a hamster cage and the mattress was on the floor. I guess they were trying to be hipsters with the decor, harkening back to the '60s era, but it felt more like 100 BC or whenever people laid their weary heads on a pile of straw on the ground. I never got an explanation as to why my mattress was on the floor. I decided it was a sign from the universe to go with the artist mentality and to literally stay grounded for my big moment. Or maybe the universe wanted to give me sciatica, and I'd focus on the pain and not my frayed nerves. Anyway, the room and the bed were highly uncomfortable, and I didn't want to sit on the floor like a crunchy hippie, so I did not spend much time there. I'd only been to NYC a couple of times to promote *Good Burger*, so I wandered around the West Village by myself, thinking about the most famous writers, poets, and performers in the city's storied history—Lenny Bruce, James Baldwin, Dylan Thomas,

Lindsay Lohan. I looked for the pigeon lady in Central Park and got a frozen hot chocolate at Serendipity3 because Kevin McCallister did that in *Home Alone 2*.

Before I knew it, it was audition time. One major problem: I had to do a five-minute set at a legit comedy club. *Oh boy*. Even though I'd circled around the cliquey stand-up scene in LA, I'd never mustered up the courage to go up onstage myself. My nerves about going it alone, amped up by the weird clique vibes, made sure I never felt comfortable enough to get behind the mic. Coming up with my own routine for the biggest audition of my life—in a week, no less—was going to require some creative shortcuts. I knew that impressions always grabbed *SNL*'s attention, and I had more than a few up my sleeve. My manager, Michael; my friend Lucky; and I spent a few hours brainstorming some impressiony bits I could do.

Stand-up on a normal night was hard enough, but this was extraspecial pressure. Tracy left some huge Air Force 1s to fill. He was so painfully funny and unique, and I knew the show wanted to try and catch lightning in a bottle with his replacement. Auditioning for *SNL* was gonna require *a lot* of courage and *a lot* of strawberry daiquiris. But I showed up, because that's 90 percent of the battle. I'd just been through hell; not much could scare me now. I was as ready as I'd ever be.

When I walked into Stand Up NY, I saw a sea of thirty Black male faces, all the guys I was up against. No women. No white peeps. I stopped in my tracks. Through a fog of cigarette smoke, I saw Kel sitting there with his signature grin. I'd had no idea he was auditioning, too, and it threw me for a loop. I hadn't seen him in three years. It was awkward.

"Holy moly, you're trying out?"

"Yeah, good luck."

"Good luck."

That was it.

I headed back outside because I began panicking about my set. All of a sudden, I saw a black town car pull up, and I realized that, no, it wasn't George W. Bush, but Lorne Michaels, who was coming to check out the night's talent. Tina Fey was close behind. Tina effing Fey was inches from me. My body's autopilot flipped on as my brain froze in shock, but my feet kept moving. I took one last deep breath to keep myself together and walked back into the club.

Kel went before I did, but I didn't watch. When it was my turn, I went back inside. The stage was the size of the person standing on it. Not a whole lot of room for physicality, my ol' reliable strong suit. I was gonna have to rely on my mental humor and how smart I could be. The reality was, I had zero stand-up material. No airplane food hacks, no Black-people-vs.-white-people jokes, no nothing. I need five full minutes, which seems like a short time but is a hella long time to try to be funny. I definitely wasn't about to get up there and go, *I just flew in from Chicago and, boy, are my arms tired!* Not my style. What was my style? I didn't have one. I was too green. I was so green, I didn't even acknowledge the audience or kick off my set with *How's everybody doing tonight?*

The host handed me the mic and I said, "Ring, ring," with a look on my face I can only describe as "classic Kenan." A little wide-eyed, a crack of a smile, a lil' mischievous. I pretended to hold a phone up to my ear. Thumb and pinkie out. You know it. You've done it. We've all done it. I had no material, but I knew I could do voices. I launched into a pretend conversation between Reverend Al Sharpton and Arnold Schwarzenegger. In my act, Arnold needed some advice on the water crisis in California. It's not like Al Sharpton was an environmental expert on drought, but those were my two best impersonations, so I threw them together with the headline of the day. I had no act. That was not an act.

I assume I did Cosby, because I'd been doing Cosby since I first tasted Jell-O. And that's all I remember. My memory bank locked the rest of that set away in a safety deposit box and threw away the key, which is probably for the best. I hit the floor pretty hard and heard crickets. I scurried off the stage and prepared to head back to my coffin of a room in Times Square to spend the night sulking and feeling sorry for myself, but I ran into a familiar face—Finesse Mitchell. Finesse went to school with my cousin and had even been to my mom's house down in Atlanta, so we hit it off right away. He and his buddy Kyle Grooms were part of the stand-up scene and both had spots on the lineup that night. After our sets, Kyle drove the three of us around the city in his beater. All I remember about that ride was me staring out the window, wondering how much rent was for each brownstone we passed. I couldn't even tell you what we talked about, but it felt cool to just kick it with two struggling comics in the big city.

Then I went back to my hotel and sulked. I felt the audition was not the fairest because I'd never done stand-up before. It was a make-or-break opportunity, one of the biggest goals in comedy, and I'd had to perform this iconic art form for the very first time. I was the youngest guy in the room. I felt immature, unprepared, and outnumbered. Almost all of those other guys I was up against had done stand-up.

I spent the night pondering and ruminating and beating myself up. I took a look around my dinky hotel room with no furniture and the mattress on the floor; the decor was meant to be artsy-fartsy, but at the time, it felt like a disappointing metaphor for my life and my career. A mess. I had to get out of there. I wandered around Times Square alone late at night, so down on myself, questioning whether I was capable of reigniting my career and even wondering if I should change professions.

First thing in the morning, my manager called: I had made it to the next round. Whoa, whoa, whoa. I stopped myself from getting overly excited because I was terrified I'd have to do a new set of stand-up. Luckily, audition number two would be on the real *SNL* stage, on a real camera. Now I could get excited! I'd been on stages in front of cameras all my life; for me it was like a kid playing in front of the mirror. This was my sweet spot. It didn't matter who would be watching. I'd be comfortable with that.

When I arrived at 30 Rock, it was so surreal. I don't even remember how I got up to legendary Studio 8H. I might have been thinking how crazy it was that an entire television show was filmed in a high-rise building. Like, how? Once I squeezed past the mass of tourists, my whole body started tingling. Inside the halls I had dreamed about for so many years, I tiptoed around as if the NBC police would catch me snooping and kick me out. The faces on the walls left me completely starstruck. Eddie and Farley were up there, barely smiling, almost like they knew that an eight-by-ten headshot could not contain a fraction of their greatness. I wanted to be on that wall.

I remember being led around backstage by television producer Lindsay Shookus. Lindsay was a talent rep at the time, who became the show's most prolific booker of hosts and musical guests. She also dated Ben Affleck somewhere between J.Lo eras one and two. Lindsay is a G, and a GOAT in the industry. She was young like me, and cool, and she helped take the stress off me and put me at ease.

This time around, I had to do seven minutes. A few days prior I had gone to my manager's office in the city and written some new material and tried to memorize what I wanted to do with my Reverend Al/Arnold material. It was heavy on improv and light on good jokes. My goal was to show I could do the impressions as opposed to how brilliant my comedic literary mind might be. I felt ready.

I walked out onstage and took my spot where so many of my idols had done their opening monologues. There was a table to my left, floating in the middle of the audience floor, under the bleacher section. The table was lit up, but the people sitting at it were engulfed in shadow. Out of the corner of my eye, I made out the very recognizable silhouettes of Lorne Michaels, Tina Fey—who was the show's head writer at the time—and Maya Rudolph. I didn't want to look over there—that seemed needy and desperate—but I could tell it was their familiar famous faces. Then I recognized all of their voices, and I thought I also heard Seth Meyers, Amy Poehler, and Rachel Dratch, too. The whole darn cast was here!

Unlike my first audition, this time I heard laughter, thank God. Lorne has a deep, guttural laugh that sounds like the ruthless tycoon people assume he is but couldn't be further from his actual personality. Seth is a giggler—Google "Muttley the dog." Tina sounds like she's pushing a "funny" button that lets out a quick, hornlike burst of "HEE-HA!" Maya laughs like a proud mom. Rachel laughs like, *Oh my God, I can't believe you just said that!* And Amy laughs like someone who loves to celebrate almost anything funny. She's the epitome of happiness like none other.

I left my tryout feeling pretty good. On the walk back to my hotel I visited several different pizza joints and let my mind wander. By slice number three I had convinced myself I could live in the Big Apple. By the time I downed the last cranberry juice in the hotel minibar, I was ready to book a U-Haul. If I wasn't going to get on *SNL*, at least I'd get my money's worth of tiny hotel drinks on NBC's dime.

But the next day I flew home and didn't hear anything for a week. Every hour was torture. I was sure I'd blown it. My initial excitement turned rotten real fast. I could hardly eat. I was already nostalgic for New York pizza. It's over; what else is there to audition for? Is there a *Family Matters* reunion special coming up that I can hop on?

But then they'd called. I'd done well, but I had one more hurdle to jump. It would be me and five other dudes. This time at the Laugh Factory in LA. And they wanted ten minutes. How was I gonna pull that out of my behind? I'm sure it was nothing for the other guys in the lineup, which included Finesse and JB Smoove. Doing an extra five is nothing to JB. JB could have blown the light, gone a full hour, and flipped off the audience at the end of his set and still gotten hired. Nobody is funnier than JB Smoove. I believe—no, I know for certain—I cursed very loudly and rattled some windows. Sigh . . . back to the comedy club.

When the final audition night arrived, I was so nervous I couldn't quench my thirst. Unfortunately, my time slot was dead last. Great, more time to freak out. I kept drinking out of the bathroom sink like a fancy dog because I didn't want to walk back and forth to the bar and be a distraction. It felt like I had just run a marathon and then chugged a gallon of sand. And not that pristine, Sandals-resort sand. I'm talking New Jersey sand. New Jersey people are salt of the earth, but New Jersey beach sand is literal salt. I stood in the tight hallway backstage, holding a paper cup of tepid men's-room water. I was up against all pro comics, who were all killing it doing their time-tested schticks. How often do you interview for a job right in front of your competition? It's not fun. *Help, I'm not ready*, I kept thinking. *I don't have this kind of confidence.* Then I'd take another dramatic gulp of my dirty sink water like I was doing a shot with Marion in *Raiders of the Lost Ark*.

Finally, it was my turn. "Man, this shit has to work or else," I said unhelpfully to myself. My mom would not have approved of my attitude or my cursing. I had one buddy in the audience, and I just did my whole set just to him. My act was so different from what the audience had just seen for the last two hours, and there was a vibe of *WTF is happening here?* when I did my Al/Arnold bit. I knew if I made my buddy laugh, that'd be the night for me. Forget everybody else. He was my focal point, and I did not waver. Oh, by the way, my friend's name is . . . Lucky.

After Richard Simmons levels of stretching my material, I managed to give an effort I was proud of. Two days later, I got the call that changed my life. All my agents and managers were on it, so I was hoping it was good news, but I wasn't sure.

"You got it," my manager said. That was on a Saturday. I had to be on set in New York City by Monday.

"I'll pack a bag and get on a plane right now!" I said breathlessly. Especially if they were paying for my ticket. "Let's go!"

I hung up and jumped up and down and pumped my fists in the air like a maniac. I will not admit to crying. I called my mom. She was so controlled. "I'm so happy for you," she said, then added she'd known it would happen because she'd seen it in a vision.

I was now a cast member on *Saturday Night Live*. I didn't announce it was official myself until I had a going-away party in LA the summer *after* my first season. It was all happening so fast, and I don't think I even believed I would last that long on the show. I was being extra cautious because I still felt my future was in limbo. I didn't want to celebrate prematurely and jinx myself. I sort of regret that. One thing I've learned is that it's important to celebrate the wins in life. You only get so many. At minimum, a nice dinner and a reasonable amount of champagne. As long as you're not rubbing it in anyone's face, it's perfectly fine to rejoice in your hard work finally paying off. Although now I work in 30 Rock and get to eat all the New York pizza I want, so in this case I am rubbing it in your face.

Two days later, I moved to New York City. Well, I crashed on my cousin Al's couch in a town house he owned in Harlem. Al and I have the same last name and we both have family in Virginia, so we assume we're cousins. We actually met on *Love Don't Cost a Thing*, and the whole time we were shooting that movie, he said, "If you ever come to New York, and need a place to stay, hit me up." I did. It was $800 a month. Perfect for a transplant to NYC and a poorly paid

SNL newbie. I'm not going to announce what my starting salary was, because my mom taught me better than that, but let's just say it was more than a greeter at Walmart but on par with a nuclear power reactor operator. New cast members sign a seven-year deal and get small incremental increases each season they stay after that. That's just what it was. Everybody had to subsidize however they could with stand-up gigs, movies, anything else that didn't interfere with the *SNL* schedule.

Al taught me how to ride the trains, and I took the subway down to 30 Rock for my very first week on *SNL*. It all just happened so fast. Four days after my last audition, I filmed my title sequence—you know, the little videos of cast members in the opening credits. In mine, I rode through Times Square poking my head out of the sunroof of a limousine, while Finesse Mitchell sat inside with a few scantily clad honeys. Finesse was also hired at the same time as me. JB Smoove was also hired, as a writer. Finesse's and my title sequences were shot by Dave Meyers, a Jewish kid who directs a lot of famous hip-hop videos, from Missy Elliott to Kendrick Lamar, today. It was a big deal; it was as if Spike Lee directed my opening. I immediately had the most Hollywood experience ever on the East Coast.

A few days later, I was crammed into Lorne's office with thirty other people, pitching sketches. Scratch that—I was sitting there, but I didn't pitch diddly-squat. Nobody told me what to do. All I heard was, "You're responsible for a couple sketches a week." That was it. There was no hand-holding. It was my responsibility to figure out how to get my name on two bits per week, whether as a collaboration or on my own. At the time, I had no writing experience; at Nickelodeon, the writers created the sketches, and I just performed them. I was a professional clown.

My first week at *SNL*, I was super lost. I was wandering around with my mouth open. On Monday they gave us a time to be in, but Tuesday they didn't. The only other deadline I knew of was Wednesday morning, when everyone had to turn in their scripts by ten a.m. Then the table read started at two p.m. Nobody called me on Monday, so I showed up on Tuesday at six thirty p.m. just to see what was going on. Everyone had been there all afternoon and were finishing dinner when I sauntered in, totally clueless. Then they all disappeared back into their offices because they'd all scheduled writing sessions with each other. Not me. I was beyond late, too late to start new sketches with people. I'd totally missed the boat because everybody already had their agendas set.

I was assigned an office with Finesse and Jordan Black, but it was like the blind leading the blind. We were all new. And Black. On arguably one of the infamously whitest shows ever. We needed a mentor, some guidance, and boy, did we get one. Huge shout-out to Tracy Morgan, who put his arm around us from day one. He even came by the studio, picked us up, and took us to lunch that very first week. We walked out of 30 Rock and were surrounded by a million restaurants. But Tracy had a special plan in mind for his mentees. We walked with him into a nearby parking garage, piled into his tricked-out pearl-colored Cadillac Escalade with the truck bed, and drove exactly one square block to TGI Fridays in Times Square. Tracy might have even just parked on the sidewalk. We could have walked the thirty yards from 30 Rock to Fridays, but this was much more exciting and memorable. I was so happy to be in a car in New York with adults. I felt like such a grown-up.

I ordered the Jack Daniel's chicken fingers, extra crispy. They were tangy and delicious. We had a view of all the people on Seventh Avenue and heard cars honking. Tracy gave us the best advice. His main quote was, "Don't peak at dress," not to be confused with "Don't peek while everyone is undressing backstage," which is a given. Didn't need to be told that. No, "Don't peak at dress" means don't do your best performance during rehearsal. Save it for the live stage. That can echo through your tenure there. If you're known for delivering when it doesn't count, you might be headed toward the door.

Tracy also took the strictness and the mystery out of our new situation. *What's gonna happen if we don't do something right or if I don't have any ideas?* He lifted the veil and made our situation so much more chill.

Tracy was the first person to really embrace me and take me under his wing. He took me back to his house and introduced me to his family. Back up. I didn't actually go *into* his house. He had me drop him off at the end of the night. Still, that's a gesture! He showed me where he was living at six in the morning. One time.

Is there solidarity amongst all the Black cast members? Absolutely. Everybody acknowledges the struggle of being the token in a traditionally white institution like *Saturday Night Live.* Do some people have different relationships with others? Are some kind of standoffish? Sure, we're all human beings with varying personalities. Tim Meadows and Tracy Morgan are polar opposites and come from different worlds. Tim is one of the cerebral Harvard guys, and Tracy's off-the-hook Brooklyn. You have to get to know Chris Rock to understand that his grumpiness doesn't necessarily mean he doesn't like you; he's just a grumpy kind of guy. You have to get to know the person, especially if it's a person who in your physical presence is different from what you know them as. Chris is known as a funny guy, a joke teller, somebody who likes to laugh. When you get in his presence, it's like, *Oh no, this is a real grown-up with kids who's lived a life and dealt with real stuff that has nothing to do with him being a stand-up comic.* Some people have to trudge through the mud to figure that out. But at the end of the day, we're all family.

I spent my first "writing night" two days after I landed at *SNL* kicking it with my new brothers, pun intended, picking at leftover takeout and wandering around the building. No work was done on my part. Around one a.m., I got tired and was about to call it a day and book out of there, when Maya pulled me into her office.

"I have this thing I think we should re-create," she said.

A week earlier, Wanda Sykes had hosted the Emmys and had an incident with Bill Cosby while doing crowd work. "*The Cosby Show*, that was all improv," Wanda said to him. "Yeah, but at least we spoke English," he shot back humorlessly from behind dark sunglasses. He was such a jerk to her. His remark was a strange one, especially as his characters in *Fat Albert* spoke heavily in Ebonics. While the interaction was bizarre, it was perfect fodder for a *SNL* bit; after all, I was born to impersonate Cosby.

Maya and I began brainstorming ideas.

"I should probably just punch you," I suggested to her.

I spent the entire week anticipating one moment. It's the closest a Black man will ever get to being an NFL kicker. Soon it was time for dress rehearsal. I sat in the wings in my Cosby costume, watching Jimmy and Tina slay at the Update desk. For the first time being at *SNL* felt real. The intensity and moving parts in the room made *All That* truly feel like a children's show. The crew effortlessly moved giant sets around, coming within inches of decapitating unsuspecting audience members without breaking a sweat. Once the lights came up on Maya, I knew we were in good hands. Whether she was performing in her first show or her fiftieth show, she came off as confident and in control. The audience was hot, and once my first line got a huge laugh, I knew we were cooking with grease. Maya/Wanda said a couple sentences to me; I said, "Get outta my face," even though Cosby never said that, and it got a super-duper laugh. For a millisecond, I was like, *Oh snap! I scored!* I wanted to celebrate but had to finish the sketch. There was more work to be done. That's when I punched Maya/Wanda out. The sketch sailed through the uprights, and even drew a lot of good buzz the following week—back when Bill Cosby and "good buzz" could still share the same sentence. If Maya hadn't brought me in on her idea, I probably wouldn't have been in that show. Aside from a brief monologue moment where Jack Black (another hero of mine) flew by Finesse and me trying to introduce ourselves to him with the quote, "Like I care!"

After my first sketch, I was off to the races! But not so fast, Pony-boy. After a stroke of beginner's luck with the Cosby sketch, I went through a major dry spell. I was a young buck, and after that first bit smashed, I got a little cocky in my head. *Just how hard could this be?* I thought to myself.

Well, the reality of how insanely difficult it actually is to write a sketch and/or get your butt on the show every week hit me fast and hard. After that lucky first break, I really struggled to get on the show, and it broke me. I remember one heated moment, a tantrum I unfairly directed at my manager. "Why am I here?" I yelled. "They're not gonna put me in the show. I don't want to waste my time or emotions!" I basically threw a fit. If I did manage to get on the show, my material didn't always work. On *SNL*, when you think something's funny, but it doesn't translate, ooh, it burns. You spend all night writing something and it hits the floor in front of fifty people. It's that raw feeling of being slashed then rubbing alcohol right on it. If the table read didn't go well on Wednesdays, I didn't like hanging around. Man, I needed some space. I needed some perspective, like, there's more going on in the world than 30 Rock. Sometimes you needed to get out of there and clear your head.

My first couple of years on *SNL* were marred by a ton of rookie mistakes, and soon, my confidence sunk to an all-time low. I tanked a bit written by T. Sean Shannon called "Randy the Bellhop." In the sketch, Randy was a wacky—you guessed it—bellhop, showing guest host Alec Baldwin and Rachel Dratch their room, except in all the wrong ways. Like, I turned on the radio and Beyoncé's "Crazy in

Love" played full blast, and I started dancing to it, instead of letting Alec and Rachel enjoy their privacy. I was excited for the first opportunity to showcase my chops on the big stage.

Thing was, I couldn't make it through dress rehearsal. I stuttered over this one line and couldn't ad-lib my way out of it. Twenty-year *SNL* veteran me would have recovered, no problem, but the rookie spiraled into full-on panic. An involuntary "Oh no!" even escaped from someone's mouth. If a slipup like that happened at Nickelodeon or in the movies I'd done, we could just do another take. At *SNL* there was a lot riding on the live performance, obviously, and to no one's surprise, the sketch didn't make it to air. Probably for the best. What bothered me most was the feeling that I'd let T. Sean down. He was totally cool with it, having been through failed sketches plenty of times.

After that, he and every other writer avoided me like COVID for a long time. And I don't blame them. I didn't know how to write sketches myself yet—mine were too weird and all over the place—so I had to rely on other people pulling me into theirs. My stuff would take twists and turns out of nowhere. I didn't think to keep things all in one setting, so there would be complicated combinations of live and pretaped portions. I started to think I'd never get a character of my own on to the show. I had no idea if I was doing a good job or not. When the season finished, I didn't even think I'd be asked back. I knew I needed to get better at writing my own characters, and prayed I'd get another season to take a stab at it.

That year, I got what we not-so-affectionately call "donut'ed" too many times, which meant having zero airtime during a show. Look closely at the cast at the end of any show when a host says good night. You'll see some crying amongst cast members. The tears you see are not happy, grateful tears for getting through the show, no, they're because they got donut'ed. The entertainment biz is so cutthroat, and that mentality breeds self-centeredness. Man, you'll do anything to make it to the top. I wish I could go back to my younger self and preach, *Hey, Kenan Thompson, there's no* I *in team!* But there's also "me," so I could see how I could be confused by it. Hmm, there's also an "eat." Dammit, now I'm hungry. Anyway, on *SNL*, your biggest competition is really with yourself: Do you have what it takes to make it through the insane pace and the peaks and valleys?

At one point I admit I almost quit because of the donuts. I was like, *What the hell am I doing here?* I was famous enough that people were trying to follow me off the subway, but I couldn't get *on* the show. Lorne used to remind me, "Don't dwell," but it took a long time to not take it personally when five of my sketches got cut the day before taping. It was a real mind game. It started to make me question myself again a little too much and wonder if there was space at *SNL* for my kind of comedy. It led to many depressive feelings.

I remember mustering the courage to ask Maya why the show's creators even picked me. "It was a no-brainer," she said. "We could tell you were ready and you're adorable. We all said, 'Obviously, it's Kenan.'" I fully freaked out hearing that. I literally had a seat next to one of the most talented performers I had ever seen. Her pedigree was legendary, being the daughter of singer Minnie Riperton and all. So the compliment sounded like it was coming from the queen and I was being knighted in service of the culture. To be complimented by someone you admire was humbling and enlightening. I wasn't just a kid laughing at his own jokes in front of the mirror. I'd been validated. To hear that the things I was doing resonated with people was heavy, man.

That had a huge impact on me and was a turning point.

I had to learn to let the donut weeks roll off my back. I'd have a week where I was in every sketch and soon began to taper my excitement; the highs and lows were just too extreme.

It took a major attitude adjustment to earn my place at *SNL*. I started being a good cheerleader and celebrating everyone's wins regardless of what was going on with me. I celebrated the show outside of myself, even if I wasn't in it at all or had an awful table read sometimes. I celebrated the miracle of putting on an hour and a half of live comedy week after week. Being on one of the most famous shows in television history felt like being on cloud nine million. After being promoted to team player, I was in a cold open for the very first time screaming, "LIVE FROM NEW YORK, IT'S SATURDAY NIGHT!" And let me tell you, that never gets old. It's exciting every single time.

TWELVE

I'm Back to Singling and Mingling

Hey, all you young singletons out there, I've been where you are. I know I may look like a boring suburban dad now, but trust me, I've experienced every phase of love: I've been the guy who always has a girlfriend; the George Clooney–esque guy who breaks up with his girlfriend every two years; the guy who listens to Stevie Wonder albums in the dark after getting dumped. I've been the club guy, the lone wolf player (with rotting Chinese food cartons in the fridge and sheets on my bed that could stand up and walk to the washing machine on their own). I've been the husband, I've been the divorcé, I've been the single dad. I got you covered. Except, full disclosure, I have not had a boyfriend. However, I will say that the universal adoration of Pete Davidson makes sense to me.

Does all of this mean I know what I'm doing when it comes to love and relationships? Absolutely not. But I can empathize, sympathize, all the "-izes." Since I'm too cheap to pay for therapy, I'll just work out my romantic issues in these pages, and maybe you'll be able to relate to my ups and downs in love. If not, then you can just follow along and laugh at and/or cry for me.

I always liked girls, starting with my church crush, and I always had steadies in high school. On hiatus from *All That*, I'd go back to my public high school, and the guys didn't care that I was on TV, but the girls did. I'd disappear for months then jump back into the mix with my theater nerds and see what was poppin'. The theater geeks shared a wing with the dance department, and I was obsessed with those girls because they were in tights and unitards all day. And they were *stacked*. We're talking about homegrown Atlanta, Georgia, thoroughbreds. My jaw was on the floor every day. In my defense, I was a hormonal teenager, and the Universal studio theater girls were hiding inside Hello Kitty and Marge Simpson costumes, and furries aren't really my jam.

I never sought to be the "ladies' man," but I did aight anyway. I started out genuinely as friends with all the girls that everybody wanted to date. Also, there's always something alluring about the kid who shows up in school mysteriously out of the blue midyear. Like exchange students. They could look like the Elephant Man and speak zero English, yet they'd have a couple birds fighting for them by the end of their first day because they're fresh meat. Exchange students are instantly famous as soon as they arrive on campus.

My brother always said that by the time I became famous, I didn't have to try anymore. I didn't have to do the things that regular guys had to do to get the attention of girls, like trying to come up with an interesting line. I got to skip all that and just be natural and be cool. The challenge for me was not trying to find something suave to say but struggling to find a woman who was genuinely interested in me for my personality, and wasn't chasing clout. But I'm not gonna lie and say I minded having a leg up. As I became an adult, and when I needed to strike up a conversation and make a good first impression, a girl might recognize my face or could tell I wasn't necessarily broke, and that has been helpful in many a situation.

In my young-adult, post–*All That* years, I was the girlfriend guy, so I would date a girl, and a year into it, she would ask me "the question."

"What are we doing?"

"What are we doing?" is code for "When are we picking out a ring?" I'd be like, "Nope, not going there, so I guess we're breaking up." And then I would need another girlfriend (because, apparently, I was codependent but didn't even know what that was). Repeat cycle. Twelve months' worth of DVDing and chilling all day/every day after work and on the weekends. Then that would hit a wall. Before you think of me as a player, I've had my fair share of getting dumped, too. In fact, after I got my heart broken one time so badly, I listened to one Stevie Wonder record on repeat, "Rain Your Love Down," in the dark. There was rain in the background of the song, a metaphor for my tears. This was around the time I put myself in hustle mode with my career, and I vowed, *never* again. I had to focus, and I didn't want daisies swirling around in my head.

For a long, long time after that—almost a decade—it was just about pimping and having a good time. A lot of people don't know that I was and remain a big club guy. This personality trait started back in Atlanta, when I'd go out with Kerwin and our boys Les and Sub. We wouldn't just go to one club for the night and be there all night long. We'd go to one club, go to a second club, go to a third club, and end up at 112, which was crackin' especially on Saturday nights and packed with Atlanta's hip-hop royalty. On any given night, Big Kap or DJ Nabs, wearing his signature beaker medallion around his neck, were spinning, Whitney and Bobby canoodled in a corner; Diddy dominated the dance floor. Dallas Austin and Jermaine Dupri held court with T.I., TLC, and a Kris Kross or two. When we'd walk in, it was nighttime, and we'd party 'til the sun came up. Then we grabbed some chicken at the twenty-four-hour Chick-fil-A (please don't @ me; we didn't know back then) and stagger into our mom's house at eight thirty a.m. By this point we were adults, so she wasn't even mad. She actually preferred that to when we rolled in at three a.m. and woke her up. As long as we made it home safe, she wasn't tripping anymore about a curfew.

I was a "hold the waller" while at the club—I'd find a spot to post up then stood there chillin' and bobbing my head to the music, drinking Long Island iced teas all night. That was my earliest drink of choice because I liked the name, and I had no clue what was in it or that it was the drink of choice of prehistoric Karens. (I've gone through many signature cocktail phases. I've done amaretto sours, Malibu rum, Captain Morgan. Somebody introduced me to Scotch at one point, and I was like, "No, it's too sophisticated, I'm not ready." And I spent years sipping Alizé, which sounded fancy because of the accent on the *e*, and is a fruity blend of vodka and cognac favored by Tupac Shakur. It took me a couple of decades to land on a straightforward vodka and soda, which is where I'm at now.)

I can't tell the story of my peak bachelor days without sharing detailed stories about partying with the *SNL* cast. When I first moved to New York, I tore the city up. I was baptized by Tracy Morgan, who took me out on a wild night that lasted until seven a.m. Nobody can hang like Tracy. He's such a beloved New York boy. He was the first mayor-of-New-York kinda person I ever rolled with. Wherever we showed up, didn't matter what time, people opened up their joint and rolled out the red carpet for him. He literally took me to all five boroughs. We ended up in the Bronx, or maybe it was deep Brooklyn, at the bottom of some church where they had a full breakfast ready for him and his buddies.

In my early *SNL* days, the cast went out nearly every night. We hit all the hot spots; back then it was Home and Marquee. We were all, like, young and childless, trying to take advantage of those New York nights. I remember once we all did this "Black Eyed Peas" sketch, and to this day that's how we reference the night before, when we all went out to a club and stayed way too late. It was me, Amy Poehler, Seth Meyers, and Will Forte, and we were so lit, by the end of the night we were jumping up and down on couches. We all had call times at six a.m. and were *wrecked*. Picture all these comedy legends lying on the floor of the writing room hungover together. Forte was face down, meaning in pain!

And, of course, who can forget the infamous *SNL* after-parties after every live show. During my first one, Chris Parnell walked into the club with a backpack and a hoodie, and I'd never seen a gray-haired gentleman enter a club situation at four a.m. with a satchel. I don't remember which club. When it's that late/early, it's all just in the darkness somewhere.

There were a few pretty awesome nights at the club with my co-stars; you'd go pass out, then wake up and go to work, and everyone is reminiscing about the funniest parts of the night. Who hooked up with whom. First rule of the *SNL* after-parties: you don't talk about the *SNL* after-parties. Sorry. I took an oath. Besides, what makes those parties so special is not about who jumped on a table and did something crazy, it's that you never knew who was going to show up and be walking amongst you.

I used to go home alone a lot, just because I didn't wanna be sick in public and I didn't want to be disgusting and eat five hot dogs in the middle of the night in front of my people. In my mind, that would be as good of an outcome as if I had a random threesome. Because I wasn't in trouble, and I had a great time just kicking it. I might get some phone numbers, but I wasn't trying to bring tricks home.

One time, I took this woman home, but only because she was beyond wasted, and wearing a teensy postage stamp dress even though it was seventeen degrees outside. In New York, when you're inside it doesn't matter, but when you're outside, within two minutes, if you're not getting in a car, you're gonna catch pneumonia. Especially when you're a skinny minny like she was. There was no meat on her bones to keep her warm. This girl was a friend of mine, and we were trying to figure out if we were going to date each other. If I didn't take her home, I was afraid of where she might have wound up. I got her into her apartment, into her bed, and she just lay down on her back and passed out. I thought, *Wow, what if I were a worse person? This would be so horrible for her.* And I realized how vulnerable women can be sometimes. I put the covers up and bounced immediately. I was so glad she was safe, but she was not the lady for me.

While I was very responsible in a lot of ways, I was also completely immature in others. During my bachelor years on *SNL*, I was still very much navigating life completely on my own. In these first few years, I was making enough to survive, but also trying to bank everything and pinch a penny. I was on TV but ate turkey sandwiches from the corner bodega and took the subway to work from Harlem. I had a roommate who labeled his food in the fridge so I wouldn't eat it. (The labeling seemed like overkill. There were only two of us. If I didn't buy it, there was a 100 percent chance it was his. What am I missing here?)

It took me forever to buy a bedroom set. I don't know why. I thought that whole process was more complicated than it was. I didn't know where to get a bed from. This was before Google and Facebook Marketplace. I didn't know I could just call 1–800-MATTRES and four hours later a new bed with one of those rickety metal frames would arrive in my home for the low, low price of $99. So I just had a mattress on the floor. My apartment was sublevel, and during snowstorms, I could feel the cold in my chest. *I'm fine!* I lied to myself. *I just need another blanket!* Eventually, I wandered over to Second Avenue and picked out a bedroom set. When I was informed by the salesperson it was $400, I asked if I could get it without the frame for $250, which kind of defeated the purpose. PS: bedroom sets seemed to be the markers of my success in my early days, because this was my second one. So many bedroom sets, so little time. I had to sell the one in LA because it was IKEA, and you're not supposed to take IKEA stuff apart and put it back together again too many times. My new black-and-silver bed was heaven, with that mattress up off the floor. And the dresser! A dresser to put a TV on instead of a mini DVD disc player in the window. That's what I'd been watching, sitting on the edge of the mattress on the floor, just staring at the window.

I didn't know how to do mundane tasks and errands. This is when I finally learned how to go to the post office and pay a bill. I was like, *I need to pay this cable bill. So I guess I have to take it all the way inside the post office and wait in line. Oh, I don't have to go all the way in and stand in line? I can just drop it into the box thing? Oh, pay by phone? That's interesting.* I learned everything mad slow.

A big part of being a bachelor is having your own bachelor pad. I left Harlem because my roommate was labeling his food in the fridge, plus they were shooting on the block, and I almost walked into it. I'd been hearing about this up-and-coming neighborhood called Williamsburg; somebody told me Busta Rhymes got a crazy loft there. Another friend got a loft and put a pool table in it, and I kept hearing the word "loft" and it seeped into my consciousness and brainwashed me and I was all, *I must have one.* I'd seen all these movies about fancy New York people who live in airy lofts, like *Big* and *After Hours.* Sometimes they even parked their car in their loft. So I went to Williamsburg and found a building that had a loft in my price range. The loft was shaped like a triangle, which would make decorating awkward, but the ceiling was tall like in the movies. I didn't end up putting even one picture on the wall, so that point was moot. I just threw my Harlem bedroom set in there and called it a day. Unfortunately, I learned very quickly that the hour-plus commute from Williamsburg to 30 Rock was very extreme. The rule of New York City subway rides is that there are no rules. I've seen people squat right in front of me and go number two. I've had dudes with sleepy bedroom eyes grind up against me in a car packed like sardines, and frankly, there's not a lot you can do about it. There are perverts and manspreaders and very loud, bad performers and even worse stenches. People eat full-course dinners on the train, which never made any sense to me. The last place I want to eat is on the subway. Oh, and your train line can stop running one day out of the blue, or worse, just park in a tunnel for an hour for no reason whatsoever and nobody tells you why. Basically, whatever can go wrong will go wrong, like, every day.

I had to get back into the city. I ended up going the other extreme and moved literally next door to 30 Rock so I'd never have to take the train to work again. I was on Forty-Eighth Street, in the middle of Midtown, so it wasn't a neighborhood at all. But I was never late, and I was surrounded by hot dog carts and Halal Guys. My apartment smelled like roasted chestnuts, which smell better than they taste, by the way, and literally faced the Christmas tree. I felt like it was my Christmas tree.

Of course, as a rookie *SNL* cast member, owning an apartment in New York City was, let's say, cost prohibitive. Heck, just renting an apartment in New York City was cost prohibitive. So when *SNL* went on hiatus every summer, I got outta Dodge. For years, I spent that time off in Las Vegas, by myself, because I couldn't afford not only a house but the taxes in New York or Los Angeles. I was still rebuilding my finances from my bankruptcy. I didn't even live in Vegas proper; I rented a house out in the wilderness by the Hoover Dam, where all the retirees live. I was so isolated, but I had a two-car garage, AC, and *Reno 911!* DVDs, so I was happy. Sure, I hung out at the Palms, but I wasn't rubbing shoulders with Suge or dating showgirls. My going-out crew were old white guys. I spent a lot of time with my mentor, this banker guy I met at a UNLV basketball game. We hit it off instantly. I liked him so much I felt comfortable confiding in him about my money situation.

"Call me sometime this week and we'll talk further about it," he said, and he meant it. I called him and we started meeting up and rebuilding my finances with a real strategy. He connected me with the accountant I still use today. I think he enjoyed giving game to a young Black kid—it probably felt like a giveback for him—but our friendship was real. I spent a lot of time with his family. We played blackjack and went to Cirque du Soleil and had steak dinners. This era taught me many practical things outside of the financial realm—like restaurant etiquette (heavy forks and cloth napkins are nice)—and v. important rules to live by—like don't take club ladies home if it's apparent they're not wearing underwear. That's just a whole lot of potential trouble.

As usual, I was on my best behavior. I mean, the first pool party I ever went to in Vegas was years later, after I was married. I didn't do all of that when I was living out there, but mostly because I heard you could get an STD from all those people being in the same dirty pool water. I'm no scientist, but that seems logical. Nah, I used the time to relax, gamble a little, maybe go to the Playboy Club and Moon Nightclub at the Palms. That was the hot spot in Vegas after *The Real World* filmed a season there and some cast members had a fake threesome in a hot tub. I wouldn't even dress up for my solo nights out. I was a local now, and locals wore T-shirts and track pants. I'd wander upstairs, have a drink by myself, realize I was by myself, not really talk to anybody, wander back downstairs, gamble a little more, and go home. I did that for four summers in a row. It was in the middle of the desert, like 115 degrees, and it was horrible. But it was only a thousand bucks per month. No roommate labeling his food and lots of solitude. Too much solitude. It was definitely lonely.

I was alone a lot, but that doesn't mean I went home alone every night. When I was back in New York, I partied a lot. I wasn't even dating, I was being an adult male and kinda smashing when I could. I wasn't quite as douchey as Steve and Doug from *A Night at the Roxbury*, but it got to a point where I was not taking care of myself at all. I'd party all night, eat crap, then pass out so I could sober up. It was a cycle of unhealthy existence, with no kind of workout to sweat it out or balance things. I also wasn't getting anything out of it, except for creepy late-night experiences. I made a conscious decision to stop being such a casual bachelor, grabbing phone numbers just for the sake of filling up a phone book. That life was so empty.

One random night back in New York, I took myself out for dinner to a restaurant called Butter; I couldn't sit in my apartment anymore. Food Network fans know that it's owned by Chef Alex Guarnaschelli, an amazing chef who is on a bunch of shows like *Chopped*. And that's where I bumped into my future wife, Christina, the mother of my children. When I met Christina, I was scarfing down Butter's Magic Molly potato flatbread, super ready not to live only for myself anymore. I wanted to share my bread, literally and figuratively. I had so much more I wanted to share with someone else.

That night I met Christina—it was a Monday. I got her number but subsequently forgot about our encounter until randomly bumping into her in Miami a couple months later. I tried to get a booty call in the middle of the night (some old Kenan was still in there), and she got mad, thinking I was trying to play her.

"I really just want some company," I told her.

"I don't believe you," Christina texted back.

She put me on punishment for a few weeks, then one day out of the blue, she hit me up. I went to her immediately, and we were inseparable for a long time. She was the first one that I would argue with and it wouldn't automatically be over. We'd have a fight, and the next day she'd be like, "So, what are we doing today?" Okay, well, I guess we're continuing to grow.

At the time, Christina hit every criterion that I would have ever had, if I'd had a checklist. She had an excitement for life, and was the outgoing version of myself that I wished I could be on a daily basis. Christina became the woman's touch in a man's life. She kept me from sitting in an undecorated house all day with no groceries in the fridge. And her family always opened their hearts and homes to me. Shout-out to Christina's mom, and her dad and grandma, who have passed away, and her uncle's family in Halifax, Nova Scotia, Canada. Wonderful people! Christina and I weren't perfect, of course, and we ended up splitting after ten wonderful years together and having two gorgeous angels that I cannot imagine my life without. I'm not the guy who talks about this kinda stuff publicly, sorry not sorry. It's complicated, as all relationships are. I will say that, looking back, I'm willing to admit that maybe I was hyperfocused on work. I mean, I gotta put my kids through college! That's all I'm gonna say about that.

Today, as I write this, my life has come full circle. I'm a bachelor again. I'm back in da clubs. This time it's way different. I've been enjoying it because I put it down for so long, I think. And I always enjoy, like, hearing the music loud, you know what I mean? Doesn't really have anything to do with the people. I get a lot of attention, yes. But that's not necessarily what I'm there for. Like, I'm there for the vibe and to hear the music loud and to, like, kind of watch people like put their arms up when a good song comes on. I'm not there to dance, even, or grind up on people, or none of that, you know what I'm saying?

A lot of nights I cut short because I'm over it. I can't do hangovers anymore. I can't overly mix my alcohol anymore. If I have four vodka sodas then two tequila shots I'm over the limit. There will be no backsliding on my body. I've worked too hard on my health to go back to late-night binge eating, which unfortunately goes hand in hand with drinking. You stay up late, you get hungry. But I can no longer try to soak up the alcohol with bacon cheeseburgers from Corner Bistro before I pass out. If I go to an *SNL* after-party now, it's one of the calm dinner parties, and that's about it, unless the host or musical guest is, like, Dave Chappelle or Jay-Z. The other kind of party is just for people looking to hook up.

Am I ready for dating and smashing and all that? I was totally fine being married. I had hung it all up and made my peace with that. So to be back at it, I could take it or leave it at any given moment. I will say, a man with his freedom back is a blessing, because I don't feel like I'm super alone. On the other hand, I'm very aware there's a slippery slope back to Looneyville. I'm definitely not trying to turn into my dad or that typical divorce story where the mom kept the house and the kids, and Dad wound up in a dusty one-bedroom apartment with bunk beds. That's why I don't love the apartment I'm in right now; it feels too temporary and transitiony. But it keeps me grinding; it keeps me motivated to get up and get after it every day to establish that wherever I do end up settling down will be nice, regardless if it's by myself or with another person. Maybe love will come back around, maybe not.

At the moment, dating is not my priority. Maybe it will be by the time this book comes out. I feel like I've done it all, except for a legit *Eyes Wide Shut*–style party. I'm dying to go. I want to see how crazy it can get. There are so many rich people, and so many suburban moms out there with nothing to do. In the meantime, I'll hang in the club. But I don't want to be the old creepy guy in the corner, either. It's hard to make a connection with somebody if you have a twenty-year age gap. It's like, all right, what are we really doing? We need to stop pretending that we're going to be boyfriend and girlfriend if you don't really like kids. If you keep sideways mentioning that you're "not a kid person" and still hanging out with me, it has to come to a head at some point.

I don't know, dating is cool sometimes, and then sometimes it's not. Do I need a chick when they're drop-dead fine and wearing some sick outfits? As far as hitting the dance floor and romancing you into liking me? Nah. I just want to go out and have a good time as opposed to sitting in my dusty crib all the time.

Love will happen again when I'm ready. I'm sure of it. I'm here to tell ya, if you want to settle down one day, I promise you will. If I can do it, anyone can. Until then, I'm okay being alone. I'm more than okay, because I know how to do it this time without getting the sads. I'll be patient and just keep my head down and work. Maybe I'll bump into that special person down the road. I'm not sure I'll ever settle down again, because it took a minute for me to realize what I wanted, and it's not that easy to find: the kind of relationship where you, your lady, and your kids can all get into one big bed together. Life is so much sweeter when you can do that.

· · · · · · · · · · · ·

THIRTEEN

Always Meet Your Heroes

Back when I started out on *SNL*, there weren't too many of those inspirational quote memes we now see everywhere online. All those motivational clichés—"You can't win the lottery if you don't play," or "Go out on a limb because that's where the fruit is"—didn't scroll past my eyes twenty-seven times a day on Instagram because social media poets like R. M. Drake didn't exist yet. Back then, if I needed some words of wisdom, I had to go to the library and look it up on microfiche! So, yeah, it took me a minute to figure out on my own that taking risks pays off. Really hitting my stride on *SNL* was a little bit of lucky timing but more really having the courage to put myself out there, take big swings, and be willing to miss.

If it wasn't for Maya Rudolph, I would have never hit the ground running. My first break was in the Jack Black/John Mayer episode— the season premiere in 2003.

I knew I shouldn't be fearing this place. With time and experience, I learned to just be happy to be at the ball. I figured out I would get in, where I fit in. My mentality became, *I'm not here to become Eddie Murphy. I'm here to be an actor.* I accepted that I was a small fish in a big pond, and I stopped tripping. There were twenty shows per season, plenty of opportunity to shine, and when I continued to do what I do, I could tell people appreciated my professionalism. No need to panic. Things flip-flop fast on *Saturday Night Live*. Land one crazy cool character and you're rooted into pop culture history forever, especially after social media exploded. Hard to believe that when I started on *SNL* we were using flip phones, and Facebook and Instagram were not even thoughts in our as-yet-un-brainwashed heads. It was still watercooler culture back when I was doing impressions of Senator Carol Moseley Braun, Mo'Nique, and S. Epatha Merkerson from *Law & Order*. I did deep dives into women from Black culture because the writers thought that was hilarious. When S. is on the case, you better watch out, detectives!

At first, I didn't think twice about playing women. I wasn't the first to do it, and it seemed like part of the job. If it was funny, it was funny. Though I do sort of regret the time I played Bobbi Kristina, daughter of Whitney Houston, played by Maya Rudolph. Whitney had been dragging her child around a little bit onstage and making her talk to the audience. That was when Maya was killing her coked-up impression of Whitney because she was off the hook at that time. As Bobbi Kristina, I wore a three-ponytailed wig, and was on my knees eating, I believe, fried chicken. People were not happy about that. "Children should be innocent and left out of things!" they screamed. Good thing Twitter didn't exist back then, or I'd have been canceled, no doubt.

I also played Star Jones, attorney-at-law and infamous rabblerouser on *The View*. Nobody else in the cast matched her physicality except me. She was an easy swing for me because the comedy around her wrote itself. She was extravagant and flamboyant and loud and a cougar. She had a handsome younger fiancé named Al (who later came out as bisexual; literally nobody was shocked), and their wedding was paid for and sponsored by all these crazy brands, like Continental Airlines (nobody understood why). Star got a reputation as the original bride-zilla, so we took the air out of it a little bit.

I did another big, brassy Black woman with long fingernails from the suburbs named Virginiaca. Eventually, maybe a little too late—that's up for debate—I came to realize that actual Black women should be playing these characters, and I put my foot down and refused to play them anymore. It was an easy first laugh, the guy-in-a-dress gag. It became a crutch, and I don't like crutches. Plus, the show needed to hire more Black women and other underrepresented groups. I got into a huge thing when the media misconstrued a quote I said: "In auditions, they just never find ones that are ready." They made it seem like I meant Black women weren't funny, and that's egregious. Why would I bring my sisters down like that? My queens! I was commenting on the simple fact that in those improv houses that are the closest experiences to doing the show, which is why they usually choose from the Groundlings in LA or the Second City in Chicago; statistically there weren't a lot of Black women that were not only in the mix, but also ready to do the show. If they were successful stand-ups, they were probably already working somewhere else and/or didn't have the sketch experience. Sometimes, not all the time, it's hard for stand-ups to adjust to ensemble mode. Hence why I had to throw on a dress and wig every week on *SNL*. Once I refused, they hired Leslie Jones, Sasheer Zamata, Ego Nwodim, and Punkie Johnson. It's still not enough.

Anyway, I'd been striding with other people's work and just being a reliable cast member. The real turning point for me came in my third season, when I was forced to share an office with a young new writer named Colin Jost. Genius move, shout-out in hindsight to Mike Shoemaker! Colin and I could not have been more opposite. He was a wide-eyed, white as snow, shaggy-haired Harvard man, and I was, well, me. He told me he'd come from the *Harvard Lampoon*, but I'd never heard of it. I knew of the National Lampoon movies, like *Animal House*, but not the newspaper that had spawned so many legendary comedy writers like Conan O'Brien and Greg Daniels, creator of the American version of *The Office*. I didn't think too deeply about it; I didn't think Colin and I were going to become best friends or anything.

As I sat in the corner, I admired his Tom Cruise–ish good looks and watched him quietly typing away or Googling what I can only imagine were lacrosse statistics. How wrong I was. Colin had a wicked-sharp comedy mind. He'd type away late into the night as I watched endless videos on YouTube and wondered if I was smart enough to be in the same room with him. I felt like the pressure was on me not to mess it up because the *SNL* world is more white than it is any other culture. I felt like he'd be fine, but I didn't want to make a new office situation awkward.

Turns out, sticking two wildly different comedy brains in close quarters was a genius move. Colin and I really clicked, we bonded over zeitgeisty stuff, and we made magic together. In my fifth year on the show, I finally got brave enough to bring an idea to him.

"Have you ever seen *Scared Straight*?" I asked Colin one day out of the blue.

"No, what is that?"

The current version of *Scared Straight*, in which troubled teens are taken to prison and yelled at by prisoners to scare them away from a future life of crime, was fairly tame. But the original version from the '70s was wild and crazy and uncensored, even though it was on broadcast television. The tagline was "Scaring the crime out of kids isn't pretty . . . but it works." One memorable quote from a lifer to a juvie was, "You know if you get up and touch one of them shoes, I'm gonna break my leg off in your ass." I showed the clip to Colin. It blew his mind.

"I want to do a character like that," I said. "Someone who yells in people's faces for no reason." Colin loved it, tippity-tapped on his computer, and, in the final version, added on the element of parables through '80s and '90s movie plotlines. The way he elevated my idea was just brilliant. We excitedly brainstormed about including all of our favorite films growing up—from *The Matrix* to *Top Gun*—and that's how we organically bonded. So many great lines in that sketch, but my personal favorite was when I yelled at an "inmate" with a line from *Teen Wolf*: "You'll be hollering, all right, because you just transformed from a man to a bitch!" I was so excited to celebrate having enough setup to get to that punch line.

Jason Sudeikis fooling around as the sketch's grizzled cop was icing on the cake. He improvised a little weird hop onto the desk, which immediately made Bill Hader break. Once we saw that, it was game on. There was nothing more fun than getting Bill to break.

From then on, Colin and I made magic together, like casting me as Boston Red Sox star David "Big Papi" Ortiz. That came from Colin—gotta give credit where credit is due. He was like, "This guy is the best. He's so jolly!" I was like, "Yeah, let's do it. I get it." I listened to five seconds of him talking, and I knew it was Scarface. Easy. But why would he be on the Update desk? He's a spokesman for crazy products. He's just going to list the Dominican foods he likes to eat and mash.

Working with Colin was like opening Pandora's box. With my first hit character, I finally started to feel like I belonged. As we did "Scared Straight" more and more and the writers put hosts next to me, I felt great that my idea was serving the show as a whole. To be able to toss an alley-oop to Charles Barkley and Lindsay Lohan meant my role was integral to the show. The self-doubt that plagued the first few seasons began to fade away, like an old scar. I started to truly feel confident, which meant learning to trust myself and the people around me.

I was able to look at my headshot on the wall, up there with Eddie and Farley and all the greats before me, and not feel the urge to tear it down in shame. I started really feeling like, *Oh yeah, I can play on this team. Everything that they're doing, I can do. And they're laughing at what I do as well.* I now had the confidence to pitch to other writers, and when I became a go-to for them, that was a monumental milestone for me. You know when your castmates put their scripts down during a table read, shift their focus to you, and make eye contact that you've created something special. Paula Pell and James Anderson were the first writers I clicked with. I knew Paula because she was a writer on year one of *All That*, along with Neal Brennan, who actually wrote Paco Delicious but got fired before it was turned into, or was stolen and turned into, Pierre Escargot. I just recently learned that while doing his podcast! I felt comfortable enough to go to Bryan Tucker, who wrote for Chris Rock and Dave Chappelle before landing at *SNL*, and told him I had an idea for a guy who has a talk show on BET but doesn't let his guests talk. That's when Diondre Cole was born and arguably my most beloved character and sketch "What Up with That?" was created. I was inspired by my castmate Will Forte's bit where he's the lead singer of a garage band featured on the local news and he keeps singing "Long Train Running" by the Doobie Brothers. It goes on and on, and he drinks a fifth of Jack Daniel's at eight o'clock in the morning. My take was, what if Diondre Cole sings his own theme song over and over?

The sketch killed at the table read. It was a giant performance piece for me, so everybody was impressed and happy that I was giving it my all from my seat. Then I had to meet with our legendary musical director at the time, the late Katreese Barnes, who put a real melody to it after I sent her myself singing into a tape recorder, "Oooh weee, what up with that?!" It was my very first time hearing it with the band. She played it for me, then we sang it together, just like an old-school musical theater rehearsal. It was so amazing hearing my concept come to life.

We continued to build it on Friday, which was also fitting day. When I saw my costume, a mauve three-piece suit with pocket kerchief, Diondre sprang to life. In rehearsal, it took a while to get it right, but I knew we were onto something when I realized everybody was sweating more than I was. They were having so much fun. Jason Sudeikis, whose only role was doing the Running Man in a red Adidas tracksuit in the background, was drenched. We had something special here if the guy with no lines was huffing and puffing.

On Saturday morning I saw my long Jheri-curled wig for the first time, and it all came together. I was ready to fully let loose. In dress rehearsal, I remember smashing it as hard as I could (even though Tracy Morgan told me not to—oops). And then in the live show I doubled down again. So did Sudeikis. He "made a meal" out of his character, our inside baseball way of saying when you get into the groove as a straight man, and you put a character on anyway. Making a meal, milking it, muggin'! By the end of the night, we were all exhausted. All of our hard work paid off, though, because the audience fell in love with "What Up with That?" and it became one of my most popular recurring sketches that I still do to this day. I even had Vice President Al Gore and Mike Tyson in them!

After "What Up with That?" I gained confidence and began checking in with Jost every week. Bryan and I had been trying things for a while, but it wasn't until after "Scared Straight" that I was able to contribute in a way that worked for the show.

It's surreal when you create an iconic recurring sketch, à la "The Coneheads" or "Two Wild & Crazy Guys" or "Spartan Cheerleaders." I've been fortunate to have a few of my own. I wrote "Deep House Dish" with James Anderson, who wrote me so many great characters that stretched me to play gay folks and women. James became one of those people that I always checked in with every week. "Family Feud" came from my collaboration with Bryan. It's just a giant talent show because everybody is doing impressions. I got to be host Steve Harvey, my original mentor. In the beginning, he gave me a lot of grief about my impersonation of him. "Yo, Little Rerun," he said in one call, "I got a lot of people calling me that I take very seriously telling me that you got me on *SNL*." I never thought he was actually going to hurt me, but he was not exactly joking, either. But then the bit blew up so hard that he had to respect it because it goes hand in hand. The more he blows up, the more I'm able to do it, and the more I'm able to do it, the more people love him, and it continues.

My other recurring game show, "Black *Jeopardy!*," was created by Bryan and Michael Che. When Tucker brought it to me, I was confident in it before I even read it because I knew it was going to be all the fun positive jokes about Black people. They don't trust the government, they don't eff with swimming pools, they love scratch-off tickets, all that stereotypical stuff. "I'm Gonna Pray on This," "Aw Hell Naw," and "They Out Here Saying" were typical categories, with punch lines like ". . . the only *Jeopardy!* where our prize money is paid in installments."

"I hope they let us do this!" I said. And then, of course, we read it at the table, and it killed. My only hesitation in the beginning was that *Jeopardy!* was Will Ferrell–as–Alex Trebek holy grail territory. Also, I've always tried to not do the Black versions of white things because that's what most stand-ups do. Like, *White people, y'all raised y'all kids like this! Black people don't do it like that!* So it was important to me to be different. I wanted the jokes to be stuff we could all laugh at comfortably.

The irony of "Black *Jeopardy!*" is that Tom Hanks stole the show on the episode with his whitey character, Doug. That was the most we'd ever try to push it politically, and it landed strong with everybody. But one of my all-time favorite moments on *SNL* happened when the late, great Chadwick Boseman hosted, and he came on "Black *Jeopardy!*" as his iconic *Black Panther* character, T'Challa from Wakanda. We were like, *Man, how are we gonna top Tom Hanks?* And then it killed because Africans and Black Americans are so different. One of the answers was about why we put our grandmama's name on our cable bills, and Chadwick as T'Challa answered it was to honor her as the foundation of the family. "That's really nice! It's wrong." Africans are much closer to their traditional tribal ancestors. Black Americans are a little detached from that, unless they grew up in a big family or in the South. We didn't know what the big payoff for his character was gonna be, but then we landed on the perfect ending. The category was "White People" and the answer was: "Your friend Karen brings *her* potato salad to *your* cookout."

"Although I have never had potato salad," T'Challa says, "I sense that this white woman does not season her food. And if she does, it is only with a tiny bit of salt. And no paprika. And she will probably add something unnecessary, like raisins. So something tells me that I should say, 'Aw, hell naw, Karen, keep your bland-ass potato salad to yourself!'" That got huge applause, and it was great because he and *Black Panther* were having such a moment for Black culture at the time. We didn't want this sketch to be the one to ruin the perfect moment! That's what makes that place such a pressure cooker: because it has the biggest people at their biggest moments. And we're usually the people who reflect what they're doing in the zeitgeist that week. Because that's what everybody's agreeing on. They know this person is there for their big moment, and here's the sketch that pertains to that.

I teach my daughters that everybody is created equal, and nobody is better than anyone else in this world, even if they have money or fame . . . but now I'm going to just drop names like a mothertrucker and tell my favorite stories of interacting with the biggest bold-faced stars and legends like Robin Williams and Robert De Niro.

I've been so blessed with so many different run-ins with insanely famous or legendary people. Of course, I do it so nonchalantly, but I don't speak on it in a nonchalant kind of way, but it's really crazy, man. Like the time I saw Brian Dennehy at the airport, and I couldn't believe how big his calves were. They're all gonna be positive stories about my time on *SNL*; I won't talk about the time TC, my favorite character from *Magnum P.I.*, told me to stop touching him at a party. I couldn't believe I was in the presence of greatness and might have congenially slapped him on the back a few times too many. I wasn't, like, caressing his shoulder or anything creepy like that.

I controlled myself much better behind the scenes at *SNL*. All these famous people wanted to be around the show. The Timbalands of the world would hang out backstage even if they weren't performing. I would turtle shell in my dressing room and just do my work, basically. I'd rather watch them from afar as opposed to, like, being in the mix or in the conversation of comparisons, like, *Yo, what you got on, what are ya wearing? Where are you going tonight?* Maybe I'm a bit of a voyeur in that fashion because before the live show, I always go to the same spot under the seats to check out the crowd vibe. I like to see the audience before they see me.

I've been on the show for twenty years—that's about four hundred episodes, and I've been in more than fifteen hundred sketches. I only know that because someone in the media apparently counted them. It's overwhelming to think about, and it all blends together. I remember different moments, but I can't remember the exact timing of things. I couldn't tell you if something happened in December 2013. If there was an earth-shattering political or news events, that might trigger a specific memory. Or if the host and musical guest were an odd pairing, like Steve Carell and Kanye West, Betty White and Jay-Z, or MSNBC news anchor Brian Williams and . . . who cares who the musical guest was, that's just weird right there.

One thing I can tell you for sure is that my favorite sketches are the last ones that close the show at 12:50 p.m. That's when they put the weirdest, quirkiest bits. Kate McKinnon did a hilarious sketch called Whiskers R We about her cats, but it was also sideline lesbian agenda stuff. It was my favorite because I'm watching my friend in a hard-core professional moment, still delivering when you think nobody really cares and just wants the show to be over. But it's like, *No, I still have a full sketch, and it's a piece of art. I'm not gonna rush through this. I'm gonna do this whole thing.* That ten-to-one block is usually a lot of fun. And don't get it twisted that it's a throwaway spot. There are only a certain number of sketches that make the show every year, and we don't care what time slot we get; as long as it's in, we are thrilled. Everybody takes every sketch very seriously.

I cannot and will not name a favorite host. I get asked that all the time, and number one, that's like asking your favorite child (Dave Chappelle), and number two, if I don't name someone (Vanessa Williams), what if I bump into them at a party and they're mad at me (TC from *Magnum P.I.*)? Early on, I would meet with the hosts to brainstorm about sketches and think that I would have an idea for them. But then I met Annette Bening, and she's so insanely gifted and was so gracious and kind and we just sat there looking at each other, and I never wasted another famous person's time ever again. What I'm trying to say is it's almost impossible to narrow this category down.

Jack Black was my first show, and his whole monologue was him running around the studio and singing and dancing and just being wild. I was so impressed that the guy could juggle nineteen plates at a time. Justin Timberlake was another insanely talented individual who could also do comedy. He could sing, dance, do anything, and he's just so likeable and gives 110 percent in every single sketch, all the way out the door. His shows were always on fire.

The person I liked the most, who worked the least, was Phoenix Suns NBA star Charles Barkley. He came in and declared, "I don't work more than two hours. Practice was two hours, games were two hours, so you got two hours to get me ready for the show." He tried to get me to fly up to the Mohegan Sun casino to gamble with him on Friday night. "Come on," he needled. "We'll gamble and we'll come back tomorrow!" Tomorrow as in Saturday, as in show day? I almost went. In hindsight I wish I had.

I love when non-actors kill it, like Peyton Manning or Elon Musk.

Elon and his little awkward self was so nice, and he did a pretty good job. He thought he was being funny, so that's all that matters. He was as committed as he could be; he was going with the program, he never rubbed against the program. He wanted to try to understand things. You would have to say things to him three times, and he would nod three times and still maybe not get it. The lady whose job it was to drag him around the stage from scene to scene during commercials had her work cut out for her.

I'll throw my two cents in about Donald Trump. The first time he was on during my tenure, nobody cared. He was Donald Trump, the guy from *The Apprentice*. New York mascot. Nobody knew if he was a racist or sexually assaulted anyone. He was fine, did a good job, typical old rich white guy material. The next time on the show, he was getting more vocal—by then he was running for president—and it soon came out that he was a slum lord and his family had super-duper-racist ties to the KKK. That time he hosted, it was way more . . . clunky. At the table read, he was a dickhead, thinking that he had better answers for everything, and acting like Mr. Entitled Billionaire. It was just before the presidential election, so it was a pretty tense week. It was right around the "grab 'em by the pussy" scandal. We tried to make the best show possible around Trump, but he didn't do himself any favors. He was reading sketches, then saying, "That's not funny. We have to do something else." He was a completely oblivious privileged white guy and not funny at all. It was awful and super gross when he offered the female cast members shoes from his daughter Ivanka's line. "I can get you some shoes," he slithered. "We're gonna send you some shoes." He kept looking us over, like only certain people could have his attention. Worse, I'd fallen off a Citi Bike and broke my arm, so I was walking around in the kind of cast where I look like Superman with my hand on my hip. I played a waiter and was in another scene playing the saxophone one-handed. But nobody noticed. It was just a bad week.

Just like during his presidency, we tried to give him the bare minimum to do, and he still managed to mess it up. We might as well have had the Madame Tussauds wax version of Trump host. The worst was when he took a phone call in the middle of a table read. It wasn't a conversation as much as it was a child pretending to do "business." "Mm-hmm . . . yes . . . okay . . . yes . . . go ahead . . . do it . . . okay . . . fantastic . . . mm-hmm . . . sure . . . okay, bye." He hung up then shared with room, "Hey, everybody, my book just went number one on the *New York Times* Best Sellers list." The call could have been real or could have been a *sad* power move by an insecure egomaniac, but it was most definitely rude. I'd earned the lucky honor of sitting next to him, and I could feel the anger of all fifty or so people in the room squarely focused in our direction. All exacerbated by the two serious-looking security dudes by the door, holding heavy duffel bags full of who knows what. I spent the rest of the table read hanging off the side of my chair to keep as far away from him as possible.

Che even dared to make fun of him during Update, so nobody paying any attention could have turned off the TV at one a.m. thinking, *Hey, that Donald Trump guy? Pretty dope!* But there's the burden of our show—we have so many unique voices in the cast and in the writers' room that appeal to a broad range of people. People only see the parts that reinforce their established beliefs—especially with social media cherry-picking bits and pieces.

All of it came to a head when Chappelle came in the week Trump was elected. We had started writing a day before the results came in, so Wednesday was a mess. The table read was completely overshadowed by the heaviness in the room. Everybody thought the world had ended. Everyone was crying. Kate McKinnon was literally in tears because she thought her underhanded impression of Hillary Clinton had influenced public opinion and cost her the election. Of course, it had nothing to do with her, but she felt a lot of unnecessary guilt about that.

All the women were sad. Everybody was sad. Lorne gave a behind-closed-doors speech once we were all gathered, reassuring us that life would go on, that the show must go on, and that now our work was as important as ever. Then Dave read a quote and we were off. It felt like we were heading into Vietnam, or the Watts riots—anything but a comedy show.

But we bounced back, 'cause that's what we do. The homie Neal Brennan was guest writing that week—we'd worked together way back when, on *All That*, when I was about fifteen. (In the time between, Neal had cocreated some Comedy Central show called *Chappelle's Show*. Maybe you've heard of it.) Chris Rock dropped by to get in on an election-night sketch, and it felt like we had something special brewing. It was like that part in the war movie when the reinforcements arrive and things start to turn around. People were reaching out to everyone involved with the show all week telling us, "We need you!" Weirdly enough, people looked to a silly comedy show for a little break from the anger and tragedy of the day.

I've always felt a responsibility to live up to *SNL*'s glorious history by trying to put on a great show every week. It's super flattering that now we carry this extra political weight on our shoulders, but I've been busting my butt every week for twenty years.

The silliest host I can remember—I don't know how else to segue out of the Trump ick—was Paris Hilton. She almost quit the show the day before. She came on around the time of her sex tape, and it was hashtag awkward. She got a bad rap for her hosting performance, but it wasn't her fault. They were making jokes about the sex tape on Update right in front of her, and I don't think she was in on the joke, because it was something real in her life. It also seemed like she was missing a lot of the jokes in the sketches or was disinterested. She did not have an easy week. By the time Friday rolled around, she had a moment where she announced, "I don't know if I wanna do this."

They call it the "Friday Meltdown." She wasn't the first one to do it, and she won't be the last. To her credit, she showed up and did the show as best as she could.

There have definitely been some interesting hosts. For example, Forest Whitaker is a lovely, talented guy, but he's intense and very artsy-fartsy. He brought his own easel and painted when we weren't rehearsing. Full disclosure about Forest: he was the original director for *Fat Albert*, and I auditioned for him and it didn't go well. They usually give you a day to prepare, but I had gotten my materials that morning. He was on me as soon as I opened my mouth. He saw that I was unprepared, and he called me out in front of a room full of strangers. It hurt my feelings, and he didn't give me the job. They gave the part to my buddy Omar Benson Miller, the big guy in *8 Mile*.

Unfortunately, the project fell apart because Forest and Bill Cosby got into an argument about something. During that timespan, I got on *SNL*. So when I saw Forest was hosting, it was a little uncomfy, and I was glad he was holed up playing Picasso in his dressing room.

Talent can only take a host so far. Many of the biggest names in showbiz, who will remain unnamed, are some of the nicest people in the world—but as professional, award-winning actors, aren't necessarily the best fit for our silly sketch comedy show. I can't count how many times a true thespian has come in and wanted to do a character his or her way. You can actually see the poor writer's face transform from hope to despair as he or she realizes the sketch isn't going to match the page. Lorne is a master at getting the laughs out of a stubborn host, but sometimes even his magic doesn't work. And, of course, being known primarily as a dramatic actor doesn't prevent someone from being a great host—look at Alec Baldwin, Amy Adams, Kerry Washington, and Jon Hamm, to name a few.

The most gung ho and happy-to-be-there host was Russell Crowe. He was on Leslie Jones and me like white on rice all that week. He just wanted to be around us because he knew we were the hangout type, the getaway. He was like a little boy, and we were a comfort zone for him. Imagine Maximus from *Gladiator* hiding in our dressing rooms so the talent department couldn't find him and make him do promos. He brought his own punch bowl and booze concoction that he made at the host dinner and that got everybody super lit. He was a family gatherer kind of a guy, with the Aussie vibe of *Let's bundle together and have a good time!* He's hyper-alpha, so a lot of people had a different experience with him, but it was the greatest week of *my* life. He didn't direct that alpha energy at Leslie or me. He looked at me as a friend, kind of taking him down the river. He's got a very adventurous, outgoing spirit.

Or was it when Halle Berry hosted? Forget about it. It's not even close. I don't even remember what she was promoting, but it was unbelievable. She could not have been nicer and sweeter and more supportive. And she isn't a stick in the eye to look at, either, the rare times I got brave enough to make eye contact. It was like staring at a modern-day Cleopatra. She's that beautiful inside and out. Am I allowed to say that? I don't want to get called into HR.

Samuel L. Jackson wasn't allowed to curse on national television, but he dropped multiple F-bombs during his appearance on "What Up with That?" I was supposed to cut him off, but Sam is very method. I was a half second late, and he actually got the whole word out. Then he did it again, and I broke the fourth wall. "Yo, my man, stop doing that. We have to pay for those!" It got a big laugh.

Making mistakes could be so fun. I remember when former cast member Will Ferrell would come back and host. When things didn't work, it made him laugh even harder. It was always such a pleasure to work with him because he's so surprisingly, shockingly nice. He's insanely Midwestern, has great manners, and is so sweet and just fully tuned in to the conversation, very present. Everybody worshipped the ground he walked on for good reason. He never had an attitude about anything.

I got to meet so many legends because of *SNL*, and they rarely disappointed. They say don't meet your heroes, but I beg to differ. I will say that Jim Carrey is a little darker and more perverted in person, even for a guy who talks with his butt cheeks. He's a freak. I'm a huge fan of Donald Glover/Childish Gambino and was so impressed with him as an actor and a human being. He read forty-five sketches to perfection at the table then in the show performed without hesitation on everything. He didn't need direction. He gave so much to everything so effortlessly. He never changed his demeanor. Like when we shot "Friendos," the short film about Migos going to group therapy, we went hard until four a.m. and Donald never complained, though Migos thought the parody made them look like "dodo birds." We did it because we believed in it, it was funny, and it was important for our culture.

The best guests know how to roll with the punches. Again, Donald Glover was a prime example. Some people don't realize how hard it is to pull off double duty as host and musical guest, but he made it look so easy. I had four pretapes that week—the most I've ever done in a single week—so we spent a lot of time together on the wrong side of midnight. When it's three forty-five a.m. and you're standing in the middle of a fake cornfield, waiting for a camera to reset, your entire body is reduced to nothing but fumes and coffee breath. Half of us are falling asleep, half are goofing around, and the other half forget how math works. Donald couldn't have been more awake and present, doing bits and working on the piece as if he was a seasoned cast member. The hype is real for that young man. He's the kind of once-in-a-generation talent that makes me want to grab him by the shoulders, stare him right in his baby browns, and say, *I love you, man.*

As I get older, I've come to appreciate meeting fans in person. I've seen enough famous people be jerks to know it takes more energy to be a dick than to be a human being. Some megastars that came through *SNL* blew me away with their kindness. Like Robert De Niro. He and I didn't speak much when he hosted, but the whole cast sent a "Happy Birthday" video message to his teenage son. Afterward he sent me a handwritten note, thanking me for the video and the week. I assume he sent one to each of the cast, but I like to think I got the only one. Let me have that. Either way, I was blown away. Robert De Niro took time out of his day to hand write a note to me! The guy who half the universe does an impression of was thanking me, for doing my regular job! Man, I should be the one thanking him.

A few years later, we were on the same plane, and I didn't want to bug him because everybody was going up to him. When the plane took off, I got the courage to speak to him. "Hey, Mr. De Niro, not sure you remember me, but I'm Kenan," I said shyly.

"Of course," he said with that signature De Niro grin. "Did you get my note?"

"It was a great note, thank you so much."

I couldn't believe he remembered little old me! Then he got off the plane and was whisked away on a golf cart, and I walked the plank like a peasant. But De Niro knew who I was!

Meeting stars at that tippy-top echelon is still surreal to me. I will never forget being in the presence of Mick Jagger and Paul Mc-Cartney for seven full days. They were close friends with Lorne, and the three of them together were like frat boys when they got around each other. Those two shows were mind-blowing. Everybody knew that Paul was a very, very sweet man. You don't ask him for things, but you can go over and hug him.

Prince was the musical guest one time, but he only did one song, when artists usually perform two. So he did a nine-minute song and was like, *There you go. That's my gift to you.* I didn't meet him, but I saw him. He came out at the end to wave good night, then ran off before the cameras came back from commercial. Beyoncé kind of did the same thing. Honestly, I rarely hang out with the musical guests. They're kind of in their own world, and the wave goodbye is our only time around them if they're that famous.

Unless they do double duty as host and musical act, like Chance the Rapper. It was the opportunity of a lifetime to work with him on the song parody "Come Back, Barack." Will Stephen wanted to do a sexy '90s R & B song like Jodeci but singing about Barack Obama. When we recorded it, it was awesome to watch Chance work, putting layers and layers to it. When we listened back, we knew we had something. We filmed the video late into Friday night, and it was raining. We didn't want Chance to get sick, so that's why he's in the back under an umbrella, not getting wet at all. But we jumped on the sword for the sake of the video. When it aired on the show, it was almost exactly a year since Obama left office and the world was on fire. At first the audience thought it was just a parody of, like, Boyz II Men—*Oh, maybe it's just a Black thing*. Then it was revealed that it was about longing for Obama, and everybody started clapping and cheering. They missed half the chorus from clapping! "Come Back, Barack" hit at exactly the right moment and captured the angst of fifty million people and became one of the most popular video shorts in *SNL* history. The icing on the cake was that it won an Emmy and it was presented to us by another of my childhood comedy idols, Ms. Carol Burnett. Carol Burnett called out my name, and I was the first one who ran up to her, and I was jumping up and down like a crazy fool. I think I scared her a little because I'm not a small guy. But I'm likeable. Carol, if you're reading this, I apologize!

Because of *SNL*, I got to meet two more of my most influential childhood idols. The first summer after I joined the show, I was able to audition for *Fat Albert* again. It had a new director, Joel Zwick, a sweet little Jewish man who'd done a million sitcoms, and I guess I pleased his palate. I was informed I'd gotten the starring role by none other than the man himself, Bill Cosby. He called me and said, "Is this the young man from the tape? You're a wonderful actor. You've got the job, kid." I remember his first line was jarring. He could have just been like, *Your name is Kenan, and I know that.* Or something less strange.

I met Cosby the first day on set. Yes, it's an ice-cold fact that Bill Cosby is an evil monster for what he did to those women. Also a fact: his importance to culture in the '70s and '80s, especially Black culture, was overwhelming. When that much love flips into that much hate so quickly, it's going to be explosive. No wonder his downfall is still grinding America to its core. But to this day, I'm still very proud of the hard work my castmates and I put into that movie. Waking up at five thirty every morning to get into that fat suit, then a long-sleeve shirt, then the red sweater was no walk in the park. They even gave me an extra-large director's chair on set to park myself between takes. Taking off that fat suit at the end of the day sure made me feel a lot better about myself looking in the mirror. I wouldn't have made it through without the amazing cast, doing bits all day in character. Dancing in my giant platform shoes.

To promote the movie, Cosby invited me to his show at the historic Apollo Theater in Harlem. When I got there, he asked me to open for him! I couldn't say no but I was terrified. I "opened" for Cosby, but I say that lightly because as we all know I stink at stand-up. I was lucky it wasn't *Showtime at the Apollo*, because Mr. Sandman would have tapped me offstage. Cosby did two shows a day, three hours a pop. He was a master, a maniac, sitting there all day with his shoes off, telling stories. It was like he owned the joint. And he was sitting there wearing a sweater with my face on it to promote *Fat Albert*! So I'm watching one of my heroes do what got me into comedy, but I just rerouted and took another way into it by being an actor. It was also my first time at the Apollo, so I got to rub the good luck log and be in that sacred place. Knowing the history of the Apollo, it was wild.

Everyone in the Junkyard Gang was a blast to work with. A lot of dope people (minus one) worked hard on it, we had a great time making it, and people still laugh when they watch it. Go ahead and give it a shot, but feel free to skip the last few minutes. Let's call it the Kenan Thompson cut.

And finally, being on *SNL* led me to meeting maybe the most important person who led me to where I am today. At the *SNL* fortieth anniversary party, I finally got to meet Eddie Murphy. He popped out of the elevator, smiled at me, and said, "What's up, man?" It was so cool to be recognized by my hero. Thank the heavens I can continue to watch *Trading Places*! When he hosted the Christmas show in 2019, we kicked it for the week. And by "kicked it," I mean I was fanboying from afar and leaving him alone as much as possible. I'm really bad at conversation when I'm fanboying; it just all sounds very desperate. I couldn't think of topics; all I could say was, "You're dope. How you feeling? We're here, we're all supporting you. Never mind the nerves; it's not real."

I didn't know how to connect to Eddie. I already knew where he was from. I don't do stand-up. He has like ten kids, and I only have two. Guys don't want to talk about their kids, do they? Maybe I can show a picture. Oh man, I don't know. All I know is I got to be in his presence for a week and he was awesome. It was a powerful week for me but for him, too. It was the thirtieth anniversary of his departure from the show. I didn't want to be like, *Oh, give me some time, too.* He was very chill and mellow. He wasn't trying to be the rock star in the leather suit anymore. I didn't want him to feel like he had to cater to every casual conversation. He seemed like he didn't want to be bothered. But he loved Lizzo, the musical guest that week. Lizzo was making him laugh a whole lot.

....

FOURTEEN

Just Like Cookies Need Milk, You Need a Partner in Crime

I was always the kind of guy who hung out with his boys. Now I have two daughters who are best friends—like, they crawl into each other's beds in the middle of the night, and if they fight, they quickly make up and hug it out. It's so darn sweet. I think about how they're going to stay like that for life, even when I'm long gone and they're grown, with kids of their own, how they're going to call each other when they need each other the most. It got me thinking about how crazy different male and female friendships are, but how important they are, no matter what. It got me thinking about Kel.

My friendship with Kel, my partner in crime, is complex. You know, true friendship between man and man is infinite and immortal. Plato said that. I don't read, so I Googled "male friendship" to make a point here, and that's what came up. Kel is and always has been a brother to me. He and I are linked together forever, whether we like it or not, like milk and cookies on a good day, or a ball and chain on a bad day. It was a short period of time, but a time that has echoed throughout my entire life.

Of course, my friendship with Kel was and is legit—we got our first tattoos together, I went to his and all of his family's weddings, and we even got racially profiled together! One particularly sticky weeknight home alone, Kel knocked on my door with a bag of laundry. I was probably just watching *Coming to America* on cable for the nine hundredth time, so I joined him for the five-minute walk to the laundry room. As we cut through the wet grass, I started to smell something foul. Something profoundly stinky. Like they'd filled the sprinklers with actual raw sewage. I've lived in New York for twenty years, so I've smelled my fair share of smells, and this was right up there with the worst of them. This shared a trophy with the men's room at Yankee Stadium, at the end of a long doubleheader, in the dog days of August.

I started to feel sick, and the soupy Florida air wasn't doing me any favors. Thankfully, the smell subsided as we got closer to the laundry room. I should have gone right back to my room, but I didn't want to risk going anywhere near ground zero. I lay down on the dryers, basking in the fresh scent of detergent, while Kel laughed his rear end off. For some reason, Kel walked us back over the lawn. If I'd opened my mouth to protest, I would have yakked right there, so I held my breath and powered through. The rumbling in my stomach even started to fade—until two men suddenly emerged from the parking lot. Two cops.

Apparently, someone at the complex had reported "two urban youth" trespassing. Kel tried explaining that we really lived here while I buckled over in pain. Kel couldn't stop them from checking for drugs hidden inside his laundry detergent. There's a joke in there about being clean that I would have knocked out of the park, if I weren't too focused on holding my dinner down.

I don't know if it was the racial injustice or the sewage, but I'd reached the point of no return. The contents of my stomach made its way onto the sidewalk, right at the cops' feet. They quickly let us go without an apology or anything. If at least one little speck got on their boots, then it was well worth it. And if you're reading this, good citizen who called the cops on two fifteen-year-old Black kids for doing laundry—please eat several dicks.

Despite all of our crazy times together, Kel and my bond was often forced by circumstance and media, which was funny in that I bonded way more with Josh, the white kid on *All That*. He was my super-close buddy. If it weren't used so much, I would say "brother from another mother," but that saying has its own Pinterest page.

Toward the end of the first season of *All That*, the producers asked if we would like our own show. "We" as in Kenan and Kel. My heart raced, and my head was spinning. We were going to shoot our own pilot before we could even vote? Two clowns, who once instigated a fight between two of our fellow cast members just for fun? Of course we wanted our own mother-flirting show! I still don't know what those execs were smoking, but it must have been the good stuff. Pairing Kel and I made sense. As two goofy Black kids with similar sensibilities, we had a natural chemistry that made things easier for the writers. We wouldn't have creative control at all—we wouldn't even have known what that meant, or how to handle it. But they did give us the freedom to ad-lib plenty. My only disappointment was that Josh wouldn't be involved, since the three of us were attached at the hip during the first season. The *Kenan & Kel & Josh* show would have been my personal choice. The rest of the cast was supportive, but I'd still try not to talk about the new project on set. Best of all, Nickelodeon decided to move the studios from Orlando to LA. Hollywood had been this mystical place, filled with Ferraris and Arsenio and $2 water bottles (which roughly translates to $45 today). I couldn't wait to meet Snoop Dogg. First, a pit stop in Minnesota, to film *D3: The Mighty Ducks*, while waiting to hear if the pilot would get picked up. I was happy to see the Ducks again, but most of all to keep my mind from wandering back to the pilot decision. One night, while I was fiddling with the cable antenna in our dingy motel, my mom called me into her room, across the hall. She was on the phone, and I didn't want to miss Ren and Stimpy getting launched into space (I was always a company man), so I turned to leave. After hanging up, she told me the news. I sprinted back into my room, ready to jump on the bed, but one bounce would have sent my head through the low ceiling. I settled for a belly flop.

When we found out the show was spinning off, I really wanted it to be a trifecta of Kel, Josh, and me. But the powers that be wanted a very direct show about two Black boys who were friends. It was a no-brainer. *Kenan & Kel* was born, and our lives forever linked.

By the very end of *All That* and *Kenan & Kel*, things got pretty bad. And a lot of that was due to Kel's funkiness. He also eloped at city hall when he was twenty-one. He got married, had kids right away, and got distracted. He moved to Pasadena, a stretch from Hollywood. It was a perfect storm and kind of turned our world upside down. I'm not going to go into more details because I feel like that's Kel's story to tell. Basically, it wasn't all burgers and slime (so much slime). On top of that, our success came with all the icky business stuff. We had to grow up pretty quickly, especially when we could see the end was near for our Nickelodeon careers. It started becoming like, *Well, what are we gonna do?* Kenan & Kel: The College Years? Kenan & Kel Buy a House Together? *Are we really gonna do this Martin and Lewis existence or not?* I was leaning toward *not*, mostly because I didn't want to be tethered to other people's decision-making. I also wanted people to know us outside of being attached to each other. I had worked so hard up to that point to be an individual performer. To get on *All That* and then get on *Kenan & Kel*, just to get lumped into a situation, that was never my plan. I never came into the game as a comedy duo. We were put together, which was fine, and we worked well together, but it wasn't like we both grew up and decided to form a band. It didn't feel like it had sustainable legs because it was a forced situation.

I became a little concerned about when our forced situation stopped working and what that meant for our futures. Would we be able to audition for individual projects and rely on our unique strengths to book gigs? Or would we not be able to work outside of each other?

I wasn't feeling the latter. I didn't necessarily tank conversations about more spin-offs, but I wasn't upset when the WB passed on three ideas pitched for future *Kenan & Kel* shows, including one that was about Kel and his new wife, and I was their cousin who was just there to annoy them. I was pretty sure it wasn't going to work, but I was a team player and agreed to go with it and see what the powers that be thought. Of course, everybody passed. *Great*, I thought, *I'm out. I'm not carving up any more ideas about this. The industry has spoken, the world has spoken, the universe has spoken, this isn't a thing for us to continue right now. We should just let it breathe.*

Kel and I started drifting apart. I was auditioning for anything I could, like a maniac, and he was a newlywed, and that was fine. I wished him the best, but I still wanted to do my own thing. We had no beef. We even tried to develop an idea for a new TV show that was a riff on *Pee-wee's Playhouse*. We faxed the one sheet about it from my house. (Yes, on an actual fax machine.) We sent it to this guy who was doing independent distribution for DVDs. It was on the early side of comedians like Byron Allen doing straight-to-consumer products to bypass the networks. I didn't hear anything about it, so I assumed the guy passed.

That's when Kel and I were growing more distant, and after a while it turned into no contact.

People correctly started assuming that we had beef. When I saw him at the *SNL* audition, we hadn't spoken in a couple years. It was weird and uncomfortable, like, *Are we gonna fill this in right here or should we just be like,* Good luck? We settled on good luck . . . and goodbye. Kel did a bit about DMX in *Toy Story*, which he has said bombed, then bolted. After that brief interface, we both went radio silent for another twelve years. Twelve. Years.

We heard about each other through friends and family but kept our distance. Our moms kept in touch, and it was super hard on them that we were not speaking. Our families were so bonded, I'd get messages of love from his people saying, "We miss you, hopefully one day y'all will get back to a point of talking." He showed up to one of my birthday parties, not because I wanted him there, but because an unwitting publicist accidentally sent him an invitation. It was hella awkward, but we didn't have a big blowout. We didn't even exchange so much as hellos, and he took off early. Life got in the way as our careers went their separate ways. The estrangement went on so long, at a certain point, there was no longer any bad blood between us, from my end at least. I found out later that Kel was going through some really serious stuff in his life—addiction, divorce, and suicidal thoughts; that's what he told *People* magazine—so it wasn't about us anymore. Things got so low, he was even the target of a Myspace hoax claiming he'd died.

Randomly, years into me being on *SNL*, Kel started doing interviews, and reporters kept asking if we had spoken and mended fences yet. It happened so often that in an interview with the *Atlantic*, Kel's publicist requested there be no questions regarding his relationship with me. I guess people were seeing my ascension and wanting to compare his current trajectory. His was more sporadic because it's a tough business. Not everybody's gonna get on *SNL* and be a part of the zeitgeist every week. He was on a lot of different shows, from samba-ing his way to runner-up on *Dancing with the Stars* to *Dance 360* back on Nickelodeon on Saturday mornings. Kel had stuff happening; he was working in the biz, but he wasn't making headlines or creating watercooler talk ticking off Star Jones like I did every week on *SNL*.

That's when Kel started speaking publicly about our beef. He told one publication we nearly reunited for an interview, but I pulled out at the last minute. He claimed he wasn't upset that I had changed my mind and that he had no hard feelings toward me, but it was I that was preventing our reunion. I don't recall pulling out of an interview simply because I heard it was with him, but if I did, I'm sorry. At first, I didn't care too much that he was speaking out, but when he started to spill the tea to gossip rags like TMZ, my blood began to boil. "The truth is," he told the site, "Kenan does not want to be seen with me in any form of media, or even have my name mentioned around him."

Another time, *All That* creator Dan Schneider was getting a lifetime achievement award at the Kids' Choice Awards, but I couldn't go because it taped at the same time as *Saturday Night Live*. So I sent a congratulation video to Dan. I didn't mention Kel in my remarks, or introduce Kel for his speech, and apparently that irked him. "I haven't talked to him in a long time," Kel told TMZ later on a sidewalk in Hollywood, adding that we weren't even Facebook friends. In my defense, this was at the time when unwanted Candy Crush invites were rampant.

It was not okay. I didn't respond to any of his nonsense because I he knew darn well what happened. I also knew from my own inside sources that Kel's head was a bit scrambled at the time. Instead of lashing out, I sent all the love and positivity I could muster through the universe to him. I didn't want to add to anybody else's stress who was going through that. I kept my distance. It wasn't time yet.

Ironically, Dan Schneider was the one person who was finally able to bring us back together. One day, he called me and said, "Listen, I don't know if this is a touchy subject or not. I know you haven't spoken to Kel in a while, but do you have a problem with him? And do you have a problem with me putting him on a new show?" Of course I didn't.

"I'm fine with it. Hire him. What a blessing you are to be offering that to him. Thank you for asking, but I don't have a problem. Do I want to work with him? Probably not at the moment." I was still trying to carve out my own trajectory.

Finally, in 2015, Dan called me again, this time to talk about doing a *Good Burger* reunion. "Have you talked to Kel in a while?" I had not. "I feel like he's changed. He told me he's in the church now."

"Oh, really?"

"Yeah, he's done a full one-eighty, as far as humility is concerned and cleaning up any kind of bad blood with people he rubbed the wrong way in the past. He's really trying to repair those relationships."

"That's great."

"You guys should talk."

"Fine, give me his number."

I called Kel, and we played phone tag for half a day, and then we actually connected. We sat on the phone for half an hour, yapping about everything.

"Yo, I can't believe it's been this long."

"I can't believe we got so distant."

"I just want you to know it's nothing but love."

Kel finally opened up and got off his chest why he had become funky at the end of our Nickelodeon careers. I apologized for my part in it, for allowing the rumor mill to take things further than they needed to as far as us distancing ourselves from each other. And he apologized for all that behavior and the way he handled it at the time, acknowledging the fact that it was not the best way to do it.

Hearing that from him wasn't necessarily all I needed, but it was definitely what our friendship needed. I was already on the forgiveness train anyway. He was having growing pains, and who was I to be the judge of how people are supposed to mature? I just wanted to have my buddy back. We'd strayed so far, I didn't exactly know how to get him back. I didn't know who or where my buddy was still, because my buddy wouldn't TMZ me like that. But I appreciated his apology so much I wasn't about to clown him about anything like that. "Are you cool?" I asked. "Can I help? Can I do anything?"

"Nah."

"Let's just go to work," I said.

Two days after that phone call, we appeared on *The Tonight Show Starring Jimmy Fallon* and did a *Good Burger* reunion sketch. And from the minute I walked into the fast-food joint as Lester Oaks, construction worker, and blurted out, "Now, looky here, Fluffernutter . . ." it's just been peaches. In 2019, Kel and I appeared on an *All That* reboot on Nickelodeon, and in 2022, when I hosted the Emmys, Kel made a cameo and we announced that we were working on the *Good Burger* movie sequel. Now that we're in such a good place, this *Good Burger* thing can happen in a smooth way, without awkwardness and jealousy. I think Kel and I have repaired our relationship to the point where he knows that even if he is frustrated by something, he will go about handling it in a much different manner. Communicating, for both of us, is number one. Number two is knowing that he's not all by himself in this.

Honestly, Kel's in such a good place now, and I'm happy for him. He's a youth pastor, and all he wants to do is put out positivity in his life. His ex-wife ran him through the mud, and the situation was a thorn in his side. It was such a burden for him that not getting along with me was the least of his issues. The least I could do was to do what I could to make sure he was comfortable, and that's what I did. I made sure they weren't going to underpay us on *Good Burger* because he didn't have that career trajectory. But I do. I wasn't going to let them pay me and not Kel. It's his character. Once we closed that deal and got the script greenlit, we both performed the bejesus out of it. It wasn't gonna be like *Coming 2 America*, where we were thirty years checked out of it. We were gonna be thirty years doubling down!

To this day, people are always quoting *Good Burger* to me. I've always loved that, but now I have the confidence and life experience to also know that they see Kel and me as individuals. It's been an amazing journey of friendship between the two of us. A real bond can't be broken just by time. A real bond can only be broken by the decision-making of both people. If one of them is still open to continuing the friendship, then more than likely it will continue because the other person will come around. They'll realize they either miss their friend or they were the problem, one of the two.

If we can get to a place where there's an acknowledgment of wrongdoing on whoever the person was that was doing those wrongdoings, then friendships can be healed. That's exactly what happened with Kel and me. And it only took thirty minutes to talk it through. Once I heard his voice, I was so happy to have my friend back, immediately. I will say, though, even if you feel wronged, you have to be willing to look at your own part affecting what went down. I've never claimed to be perfect; I leave that job to my mom. Yet I continue to try to improve my character in my daily pursuits. I strive to be a person who does not offend people or hurt their feelings. So that whatever issue you might be holding over my head, hopefully it'll come to light that that's not the kind of guy I am.

I tell my girls all the time that real friendship will stand the test of time. At the same time, betrayals are betrayals, and you cannot take them lightly. Girl friendships are tricky; they can be like a house of cards, so put yourself around people who are going to feed you good energy. It's not like Kel betrayed me, but I felt like he betrayed the friendship by targeting negativity toward me. I'm a team player. I'm not about bringing headaches toward somebody. I'm not like that. But all it takes is a real apology and proof of real change you can trust, and then you can move forward. For Kel and me, there was no time lost. We just picked up where we left off.

I never really talked about Kel's and my estrangement before. I might have mentioned that it happened and I felt bad about it, but for years I didn't explore the reasons why. I guess what I'm trying to say is talking stuff out like mature adults usually leads to good results. Timing is crucial, though. Both people have to be ready. But maybe don't go like two decades.

Today, I have my Kel and his whole family back in my life. We reminisce about the good ol' days and talk about being dads. I can't believe I pulled his baby sister out of my pants (for a comedy bit on *All That*—that needed to be clarified again), and now she's a full-grown woman and I can pull my own baby out of my pants! Our beef was long and weird and pretty awful because it wasn't just a separation of us, it was a separation of families. Now I know that Kel and I have an unbreakable bond. I'm grateful for his friendship, because our whole crazy ride, all of the ups and downs, would have been a lonely trip alone. Love you, bro!

FIFTEEN

Everything I Need to Know About Life, I Learn from My Girls

I'm surrounded by women. Amazing women. From the little babes in my household to my sister, Feleecia, to all the insanely talented women I work with every day, it's only natural that some of that positive female energy has rubbed off on me. Up until I had my baby girls, my life was pretty testosterone-heavy. I grew up doing very boyish things 24/7 with my brother, then I was attached to my boys Kel and Josh on *All That*, and before I got married, I rolled with a posse of bruhs. I think raising Georgia and Gianna has changed my life and my perspective profoundly. I had no idea the shift in your life when a child comes into the picture. It's not about you. I used to put God first, then family, then relationships. But the child part is not fourth, it's first. It's 24/7. On top of that, being blessed with daughters has been monumental.

Once I cut my first umbilical cord, and the OB/GYN made a heart shape out of the placenta, sort of like how the chefs do with rice at Benihana, I feel like my evolution into a real man began. A real man who ironically is now much more in touch with his feminine side, whether he wanted to be or not. I was a zero on the Kinsey Scale before becoming a dad, and now that I have girls, I'm like a three! It goes beyond the fact that I can do pigtails in their hair. It's the emotional stuff that's been awakened inside me living in a house full of ladies.

As far back as I can remember I wanted the wife, the big old house, and my own basketball team. It was never a question of whether or not I wanted kids. The only thing I was waiting for was the right person. And once I found that, it seemed like the natural progression of things. It was like, *All right, let's go, let's start marching down that path. Can we afford this? Yes. Well, then let's get a house and fill it with kids, so I can leave every morning for work with a thermos and a wave, saying, "I'll see you guys when I get back!"*

I was fine having girls. I just wanted healthy children, no matter what, but having girls comes with an extra level of desire to protect them. At all ages. The world reminds me constantly that there are wolves out there, and while you want to raise your girls to be able to defend themselves, you also want to be around to pick up any heavy lifting needed.

That protection instinct kicked in the first night they were born. I felt like a soldier on duty. I didn't dare sleep until the next afternoon. When we went home the following day, they handed us our baby and were basically like, "This is yours now. Bye, good luck." I thought that was a little swift, and to be honest, I was terrified. But I took to parenting like a fish to water.

See, when my wife got pregnant, she handled it. I was just along for the ride, totally into domesticating and nesting and eating all the ice cream that she wouldn't. My one big job was going to the store and getting stuff. Nobody tells you that you'll be doing that every single day for nine months. They also don't tell you that you'll buy so many things for your baby that you just don't need. By the time Georgia came, we'd used maybe 40 percent of the baby stuff we had bought. I remember I built a baby changing station then realized immediately that we could just change her on the bed. First-time parents buy up everything.

It was hard for me to even imagine taking care of a tiny little human being because I grew up a rough-and-tumble rugged boy. I didn't play with dolls. I didn't babysit anybody's kids. I never changed any diapers. None of that stuff. I had zero baby training. Once they entered this world, though, I sprang into action. And I did it with joy, even though I had dark circles under my eyes and got little sleep. I was changing Pampers left and right. I made bottles, and I especially loved bathing Georgia. That was the sweetest. She was in the palm of my hand under the sink, and I brushed her soft little hairs. She couldn't see. She was all shaky and alien-ish. But she could hear me sing impromptu songs I made up while I was bathing her. Then I'd hold her skin to skin to bond and let her suck on my nose. So many early mornings I'd get up at dawn with her, when it seemed like nobody else in the world was up but us. I saw so many sunrises and tried to take a mental snapshot to remember those moments forever.

I originally wanted a starting five, but once I became aware of the economics, I realized I was very satisfied with two. You do you, but it's the smart stopping point for Kenan S. Thompson.

Having a second child kicked things into overdrive and kicked my butt. I'm so thankful they weren't in diapers at the same time. That's one of the hardest things to do on the planet! They say there's no difference between two and however many else. Don't believe "they." They is liars! Two is very difficult! Especially now that I'm a single dad.

I remember back in the day, moms and dads had very specific parenting roles and boundaries based on their genders. No more. Those lines have been blown up for good reason. It's difficult to be a parent, especially when you're of the male persuasion! I'm not saying it's harder—I'm not playing the victim here—I just don't know that we prepare ourselves mentally for it like the ladies do. I gotta give my mom big props for handling my career like a boss, while doing every other parenting thing she had to do, plus running a household. Because kids are exhausting. They really are. They need everything from you. It's hard work. It never stops.

Thankfully, I have my mom on speed dial for questions on everything from fevers to hiccups, and if she doesn't answer right away, I panic. Who out there can relate? One time Gianna burned her face with a hair curler, and I had no idea what to do. Luckily, my mom's a nurse. She calmed me down and said not to rush to the hospital for every little thing because it'll give Gianna a traumatic aversion to doctors. See, these are things I never would think of.

My mom helps me so much, but I also feel like I have an automatic support group out in the world being a girl dad. It's really cool. Everybody's really supportive, especially to a Black girl dad. Maybe because it's one of those anti-statistics? You see a Black dude out with his girls and he has ahold of them and is not panicking and you get those head tilts and "Awwws."

"Your girls are too cute!"

"Thank you!" I say. "I can't take any credit, but they're sweethearts!" They don't need to know that Gianna will scratch them. I do hear a lot of corny dad jokes, especially from older men, who love to say, "Hey, they're lucky they didn't take after you!" or "Get your shotgun ready for the boyfriends!" Then after they finish joking, they're always like, "It'll be the best thing you've ever done in your life. They're always gonna love their dad."

Girl dads are bonded together with an understanding that it's gonna be sweet in the beginning, then it gets rough, then it gets deadly, then it gets back sweet again. If you can make it through those two middle phases, you're good.

The legit daughter fathers of the world, you can spot them a mile away because usually men ignore other people's kids. But daughter fathers miss their girls like crazy when they're not with them. So if a guy's kids aren't around him, and he sees me with Georgia and Gianna, he gives me that knowing smile. I do the same thing. Whenever I see a little girl with her dad, I'm like, *Oh my God, how precious.* It's a special club for sure.

You find out who amongst society loves a girl dad basically. And it's pretty much everybody. So many women offer to take my girls into the ladies' room in public. Or they don't look twice if I go in there with them. Because the men's room is just terrible. I wait until the last lady leaves, and then we go in.

I never really thought about what it's like to move around in the world as a woman until I had my girls. It's eye-opening. The cliques are real. The gossip is vicious, and it's never gonna end. It's like that episode of *The Sopranos* when Paulie's mom doesn't put her teeth in at dinner and is mercilessly ridiculed by the other old ladies. I don't really know what to do with all that girl drama. They are gonna bully you just because of a popularity contest or a mean-girl situation, just to be with a certain clique. I'm like, "No, don't tolerate any of that." I swear, already it's like besties with some girl then all of a sudden I don't ever see her anymore. And the parents start to not look at me. I'm like, *Snap, this is real.*

Despite all that, bottom line is girls need other girls around them. They need a tribe of women and aunties to inspire and lift them up. It's nice when a group of women are all together, thriving, gossiping, coming up with awesome stuff. I love when women pass on generational vibes or energies or tidbits. It's nice to watch that.

I try to let my daughters be their authentic selves without any judgment. I let them live in their own world, and right now that is organically very girly. I'm like, *All right, so be girly, then.* What this means is a lot of finger and toenail painting. I have not yet been roped into having my nails painted. They attempted it one time and got tired, so they only did three fingers, then they left. Which seemed kinda lazy because this little girl on the playground had a nail art machine and made a small fortune charging twenty-five cents per manicure. It was the cutest thing in the world, but I really wanted to pull her aside and whisper in her ear that she could charge at least a dollar. Inflation.

My girls love baking and feeding people teas and cakes. Gianna gets so excited when I actually say, "Yes, I would love to eat your food concoction." She's a nurturer. She puts her Bratz and Barbie dolls to bed, and she's very funny about it. Those are her little babies. She dresses them up and fully accessorizes them. When it comes to their own style, my daughters are currently in a funky phase where they wear leopard coats and baggy jeans. I don't take them shopping because I can't keep up with their sizes. And other than the side pony, I'm not really able to do their hair. But if I'm ever on my own with my girls it's tough, yet I adapt and figure out how to make things work. Like I hired the daughter of my barber to do their hair, and my cousin's wife had a girl, and she would swing by and wash their hair and rebraid it for me on the weekends. I created a little village of ladies to check in on them hair-wise. But if I have to, I'll throw a couple ponytails up. Just don't ask me to do a jumbo knotless braided updo twist crochet bun!

It's so funny how seriously I take child rearing. I love having my girls around me. I used to be such a fly-by-the-seat-of-my-pants kind of guy. I hated planning and liked to be spontaneous. When I became a father, I had to throw that all out the window. I became very present, and I try to set a good example. I didn't change myself begrudgingly. I embraced it because I just really wanted to be the best father I can be. I've grown tremendously; I'm probably damn near the most responsible person that I know! I'm so in the bubble and laser-focused on the details. Which is so unlike me.

One of the biggest epiphanies I've had so far is that you can't treat little girls and boys the same. I'm not being sexist; it's just a fact that girls are very sensitive and there's a lot of crying. The emotional energy is a little chaotic. My initial instinct was to be like, "Quit crying!" because when I was growing up, if I dared shed a tear, I'd hear, "Quit cryin' or I'll give you something to cry about!" It's different for young Black boys. If I had sons, I would very much be the same way. You have to raise Black men with thick skins, otherwise this world will chew 'em up and spit 'em out. We just don't have the luxury of not having any toughness. You gotta have it. Our fathers, our grandfathers, our uncles, they didn't speak to you twice. If they told you once, you better move the first time.

With my girls, my philosophy was, I don't want to raise whiners. I don't want them to think they can behave like that, because not everybody's going to put up with it. And you don't want to be on the wrong side of someone's bad reaction, because they don't know who you are or how precious you are to somebody. It took some trial and error to figure out that my old-school way of thinking on this was insensitive and not going to work. Like if Georgia scraped her knee and the tears started welling, the old me used to say, "Quit crying!" I realized they don't just need to shake it off, maybe they need to talk through their feelings about it. I never had any of that. It was, *Well, the pain will go away; suck it up and think about something else.* It was never like, *I'm feeling a lot of pressure from the moon this week* or whatever.

I'm definitely put in the position of being the enforcer a lot. The discipline gets extra because they always end up in tears. Kids can frustrate. I try to mitigate the frustration. I'm sure I could do much better at it, but I'm definitely better than I was in the beginning, when I'd be like, "Why don't you understand?!" I try to discipline in a calm manner. My voice is calm, and I explain my reasoning for a decision. I've learned the art of patience, patience, patience. Number one, because life is long, and number two, because children progress at their own pace. Just because they walk like a duck doesn't mean they know how to act like a duck. You gotta have that patience to get down on the floor with them or let them struggle reading through a book night after night, until they get good at it. And then one day, magically, they're very good at it.

I think a lot of the time impatience covers up fear. Fear that you're not doing enough. Fear that you're going to screw up and they're not going to be okay. They are going to be okay. I worried constantly about my daughters for the longest time. I understood why people move to boring towns when they have girls and get them some horses or something. But I've learned to calm down because now I see how resilient kids are. I've learned what the real warning signs are, as opposed to just being worried about every little slip and fall. My buddy sent Georgia a bicycle, and I thought it was way too early. Now she's just whipping around on that bike like it's nothing and I'm like, "Remember when you didn't understand what pedaling was?" Now it's just like, "Dad, can I ride my bike?" I'm like, "Of course you can, you blessed child. Of course."

Any little achievement is always mind-blowing. I remember riding around the driveway with Georgia on training wheels and I didn't have to be pushing her necessarily. She followed behind me, and we would ride around the driveway for an hour or ride up the street. That was an awesome moment. Or anytime she actually connects the bat to the ball, it's always really cool. Or when she finally decided to swim with her head underwater, because she was doggy-paddling for so long. Sometimes if you don't get them in the water before a certain age, they can get in their heads about it. Georgia was in her head about it for a while. Gianna will jump off a rock and right in the pool. She's fearless. Georgia took a while. Two summers ago she finally took swim lessons and the teacher suggested she use the goggles. That was the thing. She was scared to open her eyes underwater. When we bought her goggles, she was all about it. She took to swimming like a fish. Now she goes to the bottom and picks up little rings.

I had to let go of fear to make sure I can give my girls all the experiences in life, just like my mom did for my brother and me. So they can see all the things that the world has to offer. I'm all about broadening their horizons. Trying to raise them to be good citizens of the community and, you know, thoughtful and all that kind of stuff. How to behave in restaurants. Just living in New York City most of the year, when I'm taping *SNL*, they are exposed to so much. They are surrounded by people from all walks of life, and there are a million cultural things to see and do. I just gotta find the time to do it all. I do know parents of a ten-year-old who let her take the bus and subway by herself. That's bananas. I'm nowhere near that yet.

Home life is a beautiful thing. The whole family-man thing of it all kicked right in, and it's been an amazing ride. I love living with my girls. I love putting up piñatas every year for their birthdays. I love it all. I definitely am a guys' guy. But I enjoy nice surroundings and good smells. I think a dad in a house full of women is definitely a man to be looked up to because women hold people around them to higher standards. I've grown and matured in ways that I never imagined, all because of my beautiful little angels. I never want to let them down.

SIXTEEN

For Those Who Made Me Laugh, I Salute You

From Jimmy Fallon in my first year way back in 2003, to newbies like Bowen Yang today, I've seen the world's greatest comedy talent come and go. Name your favorite *SNL* cast member, and I've got an incredible story. I can't tell them all—that could be its own book—so I'll just spin some yarns stream-of-consciously:

Let's start first with Lorne Michaels, the man, the myth, the legend. He's subdued and laid-back, but he represents so much—what he can do, what he has done. Working with Lorne is like staring at the edge of a sword. He does Jedi mind tricks before the show to rattle you. He'll say something like, "There's a lot at stake here." But then you go out there and overperform and kill it, and he's standing in the wings with a sly grin on his face. He's like a coach. He knows how to get the best out of you.

Lorne has always been protective of me and thinks of me as one of his kids. We have a great relationship; he's said insanely complimentary things about me in the press. Every time he walks past me, he taps me on the arm. That way I know I'm in good enough graces and I'm not just a ghost on the wall. That's enough validation for me to do my job. But all of our run-ins are usually pretty short and sweet, only because in my mind he's insanely busy and he's also heard every joke attempt there ever has been. Even though he loves to laugh and loves people that make him laugh, it feels like a very daunting task. So I'm always a deer in headlights a little bit around him.

I got more comfortable around Lorne in year seventeen. He's invited me to his house and to Yankee games. But I try to keep it professional. The bottom line is, are you gonna be best friends with the Wizard of Oz? I don't think so. Let that man stay behind the curtain.

When I landed at *SNL*, Jimmy Fallon might as well have been Adam Sandler; he was a bona fide rock star. In the pitch meeting, he was the guy who kept the energy up. Everybody wanted to be his friend. Jimmy is so quick, his comedy mind is so sharp, and he has references that are deep—they go way back. He is a comedy student for real. In the early days, his looks might have garnished him attention, and then he spent a lot of time on Update, which doesn't really showcase his true abilities. You can see from his skits on *The Tonight Show* that he's a real performer on another level. He's the Mick Jagger of *SNL*.

I watched Andy Samberg come and go. I remember watching his audition while I was shooting *Snakes on a Plane* in Vancouver. Andy was an obvious choice. I was like, *Oh, that kid's a rock star.* He had the looks, and he had a very confident sense of what he thought was funny.

He's very silly, and that's his main thing: to be the goofball. The whole handsome thing is his burden, if you will. People just want to look at him as a pretty boy, but he's really elevated goofiness. Andy is a student of the smart version of as dumb as you can be, like Conan O'Brien: be smart and dumb at the same time. He's also the pioneer of *SNL*'s digital shorts. "Threw It on the Ground" is, like, probably one of my most favorite things ever. That mixture is perfect. Can't go wrong with lyrics like, "Man, this ain't my dad. This is a cell phone. . . . What you think, I'm stupid?"

Andy auditioned with Bill Hader. It's so funny because his normal speaking voice is so different from his performing voice. He just flips confidently into a completely different character. Bill is also a movie head, so he is like a film database. He's seen every movie.

Both Andy and Bill are insanely endearing and charming, and I love them both. Fred Armisen has made me laugh like no other, genius! Bobby Moynihan is the kindest and one of the funniest people I've met. So many laughs together, his brain is like an encyclopedia. He remembers every good story! Taran Killam is one of the greatest performers I've ever seen, and Jay Pharoah is the true king of impressions.

Colin Jost likes to sweat it through the night. He writes better when he is under pressure, so he likes to procrastinate. I've watched him do this for eight years. His responsibilities were to write for the show and a bunch of other people. But sometimes here and there he'd write for me because he knew I could score. So if he was teetering on something and not really sure about it, he would just write it around me or put me in it and I would deliver.

Sharing an office with Colin was the best. I never went to college, so he felt like my first college roommate in a dorm room. He did his thing, and I did my thing, and we sat with our backs to each other in comfortable silence but always turned around at the right time to talk. I made sure to wear headphones if I wanted to listen to a video so as to be cordial. He'd be running around doing his own thing a lot, but then we had fun together in our cozy little space, too.

When he became a head writer he got his own office. So that was it. But neither one of us will ever really forget our time together. We're still hyperclose to this day. One more thing about Colin. He's a sweet and humble guy, even still after his blossom into a Hollywood stud.

Michael Che, forget about it. Che is the GOAT, man. Like, that dude is our generational GOAT. Che is prolific, and there hasn't been any other Black head writer in my era. You can always pick out a Che bit because it's very much in the current culture but witty enough to be formulated into comedy.

Che also has no desire to cross over to the cast—he hates doing sketches. He'd rather be puppeteering and getting his message out through the bits he writes for others. I'll never forget how he wrote me into the "Blackpack" monologue Eddie Murphy performed as host in December 2019. Che didn't have to do it—it was fine with just Dave Chappelle and Chris Tucker and Tracy Morgan, but Che was adamant that it include a current cast member and put me in. He could have easily written himself into the monologue, but he didn't. Shoutout to Che for selflessly throwing me in a monologue with those four greats of comedy, my comic heroes. Che enjoys writing for me, and I appreciate the faith he has in me. Sometimes, he'd just come up to me before the table read and say, "Hey, I wrote this thing," and walk away because he knows I got it.

Jason Sudeikis has a level of confidence that is pretty rare amongst our weird, quirky, neurotic little sketch comic circle. I've never seen him afraid of any moment or afraid of processing any idea to see whether or not it's funny or has legs. He spent a year writing before he crossed over to the cast, so he understood how to break down premise. He also played college basketball, so he is very alpha. When he involves himself in your sketch, he'll find what works and run two hundred miles an hour in that direction. He is the king of finding hidden gems and making the most of his character, even if it's just the way he adjusts his belt buckle. You can't write that. He has great presence.

And a great eye for talent. Jason is the one who first pointed out to me how genius Kristen Wiig was as a performer. Comedy wasn't even her first thing, which just shows how much of a natural she was. In her first week, Sudeikis nudged me and was like, "Watch this. Wiig is crazy funny." And Kristen ran with the sketch. From the beginning, she was doing comedy at a super-high level. Jason championed Wiig; he knew she was a force, and he was the first one to write with her and put up characters every week. "Two A-Holes" came out of that. We all saw Kristen blossom into this fearlessness, when people hit their sweet spot and start firing on all cylinders. All of a sudden she was in everything. But not long after, she was gone, and had left the show for other opportunities.

Then all of a sudden, Kate McKinnon was there, and we could see that Kate was a force, too, also different and quirky and hilarious but equally fearless. Watching her arc was amazing. She had the balls to be like, "Hey, maybe I can do Rudy Giuliani!" Fantastic. She knew how to master the room. And whenever people do that, they become the names we know, the Molly Shannons, the Gilda Radners. They become those household names for commanding the room in a way that's creative, new, entertaining, and frequent. She became that.

By the way, anyone who says women aren't funny are brain-dead. I'm all about women who make me laugh. I mean, when you've worked with Kate, Kristen, Cecily Strong, Aidy "Solid as a Hammer" Bryant, Amy Poehler, Tina Fey, Maya Rudolph, amongst so many others, c'mon! It's such a blessing that they all take on the role of my "older" sisters. They have all had my back and helped me along the way. They've treated me like their younger brother, and I don't know if they knew that I was watching them twice as hard as anyone else, learning from them twice as hard, and wanting to praise them twice as much. I give them all the credit in the world because I came in witnessing real pros operating at such an elite level. Amy was scoring so hard, and it was only like her fourth or fifth year. And Tina was the most prolific writer there in history.

Tina's the one you want to impress, and Maya's the matriarch, the one that everybody wants the love from. Everybody adores her children, and I'm in awe of the symbiotic relationship she seems to have with her husband, Paul Thomas Anderson. That's couple goals, for real. Maya, too, nurtured me and treated me like her baby brother. I used to just love to make her laugh and loved listening to her at the table whenever she would have to sing something. She's a songbird and has an incredible God-given voice, just like her mother. Sitting next to her during table reads, I knew I was blessed to be such a close witness to her greatness.

Seeing Tina and Amy discover that they worked well together was inspiring! Their relationship reminded me of my thing with Kel because they both were very good at their individual things but also got lumped together a lot. Tina was great at Update and writing other sketches. And Amy was a powerhouse performer. They were a two-headed dragon—the brainiac and the maniac.

My favorite brain is Cecily's—she's insanely quick and insanely funny because she is another one who is super silly, but her comedy is very surreal. She has a way of blending those two elements together in a way that you don't feel like left out of her brilliance. She's kind, smart, quick-witted, but just layered and deep and sweet and gorgeous. She's a goddess, Maya's a goddess, they're both goddesses in my eyes. Maya was my original sister, but she ended up leaving quickly-ish. Cecily I see almost as my child because she came in behind me and she would sing in the band behind me and I watched her ascend to the heights of everything. She is one of the funniest people on the planet.

One of my best friends in the world is Leslie Jones. She came into the cast right after my Black-women-in-comedy controversy. The real quote was, "They just been having a hard time finding people that are ready to do the show." They took that and made it, like, "I think Black women ain't funny." I'm like, where do you get that from that? Leslie was kind of firing off in the media, like, "If that's what that mother-fucker said, I know he don't want it with me 'cause I'll burn his ass up." Very confrontational. The first time I met her, she looked me up and down, sized me up, and said, "Did you really say that fucked-up shit?" and I looked her straight in the eye and said, "No," and within two seconds, we just were kicking it and having fun laughing. We are so close, it's crazy. We laugh all day long because we have a lot in common.

She tells me I remind her of her brother, who passed away. We both appreciate the value our siblings brought to our lives. I love being around people who make me laugh really hard, and it just naturally happens between us. Leslie's and my senses of humor and thought processes are aligned, as far as what we might find ridiculous or would spark a laughing fit.

Our relationship is deep. Leslie feels like a blood sister because when she's upset, I'm upset, and vice versa. She was my everyday kicking-it partner, man. To this day, I'm always at her house when I go to LA. We hang out and chat. She's my strong female buddy, and I support her because it's hard on Black women out there. I have a protective kind of thing over her as a Black woman up against the grain. Whatever she does, there's always crazy comments or people try to bully her just because people attack tall people, whatever it is. I always want to be there for her as long as she's on the right side of the conversation. Ninety-nine times out of a hundred, she is.

I'm also really tight with Pete Davidson. He is such a sweet boy; he doesn't have a malicious bone in his body. I don't think he wishes harm on anybody. He might have a temper, but he's a six-foot-tall Italian who loves his momma! So of course he has passion and fire. We used to laugh about the dumbest stuff in the hallways. We used to sing the cast names of *Franklin & Bash* like Bill Cosby because they're all kind of weird, like Mark-Paul Gosselaar, Malcolm McDowell, Kumail Nanjiani, and Breckin Meyer. Since he left the show, we continue to text each other and try to stay connected. But it's sad, you know, because you don't have your play friends around every day, six days a week, like it used to be. And you try not to take it for granted, but it's so many long hours, and it's so much stress.

When you're in the thick of it, you never think you'll see the end of the Kate McKinnon era or the Andy Samberg era. When cast members come on the show, you don't think about the day they're going to leave. It's like when you buy a puppy, you don't think about its life span. You just enjoy having it for as long as possible. It's inevitable that my coworkers, my friends, are going to move on with their lives. After twenty years on the show, I've been through it so many times, but it never gets any easier. The day comes when it's their last show. And you watch them take their last breath before their final moment on the show, after spending so much blood, sweat, and tears making people laugh. It's emotional. When it's time to say goodbye, it's a hypertearful moment.

I don't feel lost without them when they leave necessarily. It's just sad that their physical presence is no longer 90 percent of my week. It's always very, very painful. And I usually compartmentalize it, because it happens so fast. The last Sunday of the season, all of a sudden, you're not at 30 Rock 24/7. By the time you come back a couple months later, everything's different—you never have that amount of time with those people again. They go off in their life, and they have marriages and kids and buy houses. Some people you'll see, but some, three, four, five years will fly by and you'll be like, "I haven't seen you in so long because you've been busy" or "I've been busy!" Time slips through your fingers.

We're so entrenched within each other's lives and then, all of a sudden, poof, they're gone. It's so intense. When Maya left, I was crushed. She was my happy place, my comfort zone. I felt kind of tucked underneath her and watched how people treated her at the show and at the after-parties. Seeing all the famous people coming up to her demonstrated her profound impact on the show. And when she left it was like, *Well, I guess I'm the little brother flying solo.*

In a perfect world, you wouldn't leave your family, you continue to go on living together forever. But that's not the reality of *Saturday Night Live*. It's been hard to be the one left behind, but at the same time, I have zero regrets being the longest-running cast member ever on *SNL*. The things I've seen and done, and the people I've met, are priceless. Imagine looking around the table and going down that list of alumni names. I've watched the best and the brightest create and perform iconic material and characters that will stand the test of time. I've been lucky enough to see the experts up close. I've seen Tina Fey perfect sketches in record time under pressure. I've seen countless people try and fail to get Fred Armisen to stop doing bits. I like to think that I've been around enough experts in my career that a little of their magic dust has rubbed off on me.

On a day-to-day basis for the last two decades, I've gotten to laugh with the greatest comedians of our time. And I'm considered one of them now, too. I feel so lucky to have had a front-row seat on one of the greatest shows in television history.

A Change Is Gonna Come. Probably.

Five seasons of *All That*, four seasons of *Kenan & Kel*, and twenty-ish seasons of *Saturday Night Live* will put some comedy hairs on your chest. I've had a good, long run on *SNL*. I went from almost quitting the show in my rookie years to cowriting "Come Back, Barack," which still might single-handedly bring Obama out of retirement one day. Only time will tell.

A few years into *SNL*, one of the writers, Bryan Tucker, pointed out this recurring stage direction being slipped into a script: *KENAN REACTS*. Then I started noticing it pop up more and more frequently. Apparently, the writers got used to this as a way of, as they so kindly put it, "saving their sketches." People laugh at me reacting to stuff, and I like making people laugh, so I roll with it. There are worse things to be known for. Like hiding hundreds of unworn women's panties in your ceiling.

I've won an Emmy. I've hosted the Emmys and rubbed shoulders with Jeff Bezos and Oprah. I may have even told them that I loved them. I've received a star on the Hollywood Walk of Fame, right next to Lorne Michaels and *The Honeymooners* star Art Carney, which is so cool. I've accomplished more in my life so far than I ever thought I would in my wildest dreams. But you always have to set new goals for yourself; otherwise, what's the point of life?

I've been making people laugh now for a longer time than I spent in actual school, and I'm proud of every minute. But lately, after two decades on *SNL*, I'm kind of farming for new material and ways to stay fresh. Friends, it could be the end of an era. I promised myself I would make it to twenty years, but by the time this book comes out, I might be on my last season. It's bittersweet, but change is good. Billie Eilish hit a wall when she changed her hair. I get that and the fact that people live their whole lives thinking Woodstock was the greatest thing ever. Some people wanted to freeze me on *All That* because it was the best times of *their* lives. But we gotta allow people to find themselves and grow, as opposed to holding on so tightly to a moment in time.

My philosophy is to just keep pushing forward because, not to freak anybody out, but life goes on, you know what I'm saying? My future goals include:

1. Being in the mix and be on those power lists like Tyler Perry. I don't need to have a whole studio built, but if someone wants to acquire my company for $900 million like Reese Witherspoon, I'm good with that. I look at guys like Steven Spielberg, David Geffen, and Clarence Avant as inspiration. These guys that have their finger on the pulse of creativity, but also the zeitgeist of society. It would be my dream to build a Dreamworks and make movies. Comedy will always be close to my heart, you know. But I think the movies that live with us the longest are coming-of-age genre, like the *Sandlot*s and the *Mighty Ducks* and the *Good Burger*s of the world. That's a very sweet spot for American cinema. Then I'd sell my production company, you know, several times.

2. Getting back to my roots doing theater. I haven't done much the-

ater since my early days with Freddie Hendricks in Atlanta. Once I started working for the big checks, that's kind of how it stayed. I went to see James McAvoy do *Cyrano* on Broadway three times. It's an incredible amount of words. He's so good. I would really have to train for a while to be able to remember all that. I mean, talking for three hours?

3. Playing my guitar. I'm obsessed with learning musical instruments these days. I just need to find time to practice. I'm sure I could still put it back together on the trumpet, but it's hard on the mouth, and you know the ladies like soft lips.

4. Maybe I'll invent something like the Cabbage Patch Kids, or I could just be friends with the guy or gal who creates a Cabbage Patch Kids. Either way. Because that could get you a condo downtown with two spiral staircases in it like the Cosby house. I still haven't reached that goal, and I will stop at nothing to achieve it.

5. Go to an *Eyes Wide Shut* party. It's gotta exist somewhere. Maybe I'm kidding, maybe I'm not.

6. Mentor young actors. I didn't get my comedy training at improv theaters like the Second City in Chicago or the Groundlings in Los Angeles. And I still made it, carving my own path. Just like Freddie Hendricks did for me, I'd like to share all I know about my craft with some up-and-comers. I may be an old pro, but I still get a belly full of butterflies. I've found that it's better to shake them instead of letting them shake me. I do a warm-up song to heat up the crowd before each show that does the trick. Before I could even drive a car, I learned that most sketches work with a straight man (or a gay woman, it's the twenty-first century) playing off a "weird thing." The straight man reacts to the weird thing the same as the audience does. A white "Black *Jeopardy!*" contestant agrees with his competition? Straight man is pleasantly surprised. Two drunk dirtballs swapping spit at last call? Straight man is grossed out.

Hundreds of unworn women's underwears fall out of your grandfather's ceiling? Straight man is shocked, confused, and mildly intrigued. You get it. Whether I'm playing the weird-undies grandpa or the straight man, I just want everyone to score. At this point in my career, I'm like Showtime-era Magic Johnson. Sure, I could try and hit a home run every game, but I want my teammates to get touchdowns, too. It elevates the whole show. Are you confused by the mixed sports metaphors yet? Congrats! You just played the straight man!

7. Stay ambitious. One thing I learned early on: It's hard for a young person to lean into ambition. It feels unnatural, like trying on a fancy shirt at some high-end store you shouldn't even be allowed inside. All it takes is one glance in the mirror at how fresh you look to realize this shirt could be the key to landing that job or winning over that girl or earning the keys to that car of your own. Ambition is what separates the dreamers from the doers. Not all young people know what exactly they should be striving for, and that's okay, too.

8. Pay attention to the things people tell you you're good at—whether it's running, shooting a basketball, singing, making people laugh, being the dude who holds that bulletproof shield on the SWAT team, whatever. Do that stuff over and over again until you know you can stand to do it for a lifetime, and then go do it even harder. People have been telling me since I was five that I should perform, so I kept doing it, and kept on doing it, until I didn't need anyone to tell me anymore. The universe likes to give out hints. All you have to do is slow down for a minute and listen.

9. Be an elder statesman and give back to the next generation. I like to think I've taken each new cast member under my wing and helped make them comfortable, but everyone that gets hired is already so talented. I want to go directly to the source. With the

help of my good friend Cherie, we've set up a nationwide talent search for the next stand-up comedy stars, a few years running now. The winners also get to visit me backstage at *SNL* for a show and watch how the sausage is made. Even as a regular on *SNL Jr.*, I was totally in the dark when I got here. There's nothing like it. I wasn't from New York, and I didn't come from any of the big improv houses, so I had no idea how anything worked behind the scenes—the size, the scale, where it even was, it was all a mystery. I want to give potential rising stars a heads-up, so maybe their auditions can be a little less stressy than mine was. When I do pass the torch someday, I'll be able to kick back and relax, knowing the show will be in good hands for the next forty-four years and beyond.

10. Focus on my family. As a proud daddy to two perfect little girls, that's number one. Animated projects come along, and while I do love messing around in the booth, I mainly do it for the girls. I have eight years of college to prepare for, and way more if we're raising secret doctors or lawyers or astronauts. I hear astronauts are drowning in student debt these days. As much as Georgia enjoys laughing at a goofy hedgehog that sounds suspiciously like her daddy, it's all going straight into the bank.

So those are some things I'm thinking about doing once I leave *Saturday Night Live*. Then again, who knows? I might just stay on the show until I keel over dancing and singing to "What Up with That?" and the special guest is all twelve of Nick Cannon's fully grown children. Or maybe I'll go behind the scenes. With twenty years under my belt, I'm more empowered to speak up than I used to be. Even if I have a one-line walk-on in a sketch, I pay close attention to see if there are any lines or blocking that need tweaking. During rehearsal, if I notice a wide shot that should be a close-up, or if the camera is missing an important setup or punch line, I'll ask the director or stage manager what they think. When I first started, I had no idea what the heck was going on, I was just along for the ride, so it feels good to have grown into an authority in 8H. Next season you might even catch me spell-checking the cue cards with Wally, our cue card guy for the last twenty-eight years.

When Gal Gadot hosted, we did this hilarious first date sketch. She played a foreigner who knew nothing about American culture in the '90s. As Gal's guy, I played OJ Simpson, absolutely tickled by the fact that this woman had no idea who he was or what he had (allegedly) done (that week, OJ had been released from jail, so he was still topical, over a decade after the whole white Bronco thing). Originally, the script had jokes mentioning Nicole Brown and Ron Goldman. Even twelve years later, we were walking a tightrope. These people actually lost their lives in real life. Out of respect, I thought we should leave out references to the victims and stick to the present reality that OJ Simpson is freely walking around somewhere, swiping on dating apps and enjoying fancy steak dinners. I brought my concerns up at rehearsal, and we all agreed. The jokes were cut, and the sketch still destroyed.

On that note: with great power comes great responsibility. I know that quote off the top of my head because it comes from *Spider-Man*. Being on *SNL* every week, I feel a moral obligation to use this enormously influential platform in a responsible way. I'm extremely proud of sketches like "Black *Jeopardy!*" and being part of Dave Chappelle's shows, which has a lot of good, conscious activity. I, a Black man, wore a monkey suit in a Mario Brothers sketch, and we pulled it off. I survived the barrage of hostility from both sides of the aisle. "Scared Straight" pushed the envelope in terms of displaying stereotypical characters. The Black prison guard has a du-rag on, but he's spouting off '80s movie plots. Now you associate that image with laughter instead of a carjacking on the nightly news. There's more complexity to the cover of the book. If we can't push it on the most famous sketch comedy show in history, then who can?

So yeah, maybe I'll stick around. A man's got a right to change his mind. Besides, I never said I was leaving for sure. The media said that. All I've ever said was that I wanted to make it to twenty years. I'll definitely be there for the fiftieth anniversary, and it's an ongoing conversation after that. Why would I ever leave if I'm not in anybody's way? The goal every year is to be asked back by the end of the summer. I love *Saturday Night Live* almost as much as I love my mama. Being in one spot allows for a whole lot of family time, and my girls deserve that. Those mornings where we get to walk to school together, and I can pick them up when I'm off, bookend the day. That is vital. Maybe I will stop performing one day but stay on the show in some other capacity. If Lorne ever retires and his job opens up, that salary would definitely get me at least two spiral staircases!

Acknowledgments

So many people and places to thank, so little time! First and foremost, my mom, dad, brother, and sister . . . actually, my entire family, all the way back to our Virginia roots! My Atlanta family, you know who you are, and if you don't know who you are, you might want to get that checked out by a doctor.

I wouldn't be the finely educated young man I am today without the amazing schools I attended as a kid—KinderCare, Old National Christian Academy, Woodward Academy, and Tri-Cities High School. And I wouldn't be the actor I am today without my earliest theater training and the life-changing mentors I've been blessed to cross paths with my entire life: Union City Theater, Alliance Theatre, Seven Stages Theatre, the Youth Ensemble of Atlanta (YEA), Freddie Hendricks, Thomas Byrd, and Brian Robbins and family.

Shout-out to my hard-working business team: My manager, Michael Goldman; all my agents I've ever had the pleasure of working with, including my current team at United Talent Agency, led by Nancy Gates, Nina Shaw, Gordon Bobb, Michelle Parelle, and the rest of my law team.

Let's go with everybody I've ever worked with, including but not limited to: Michael Aloian; Kyle Mosley and family; Sub Les Tani Marole and our whole Greidiens team; Nickelodeon, Paramount, Viacom, and Disney (my *Mighty Ducks* family); Illumination and my

Grinch family; and my *Trolls* family! It's been a long, fulfilling career! I got a lot of work families to thank!

Lorne Michaels and the whole *SNL* and NBCUniversal family!

The team that helped put this book together: my intrepid collaborator Dibs Baer, thanks for talking to me while I was on a boat, on a sidewalk in front of DUMBO House, during a haircut, at the gas station, and while brushing my teeth. My dedicated and dogged literary agent, Albert Lee, the biggest and best reason this book is in front of your eyeballs.

The staff at HarperCollins: Kate D'Esmond, Katie O'Callaghan, Alicia Gencarelli, Michael Siebert, Beth Silfin, Kyle O'Brien, Milan Bozic, Liz Velez, and my superstar editor, Adenike Olanrewaju.

And last, but definitely not least, my adorable angel babies, Gianna and Georgia, who have inspired me and taught me more than anyone else on this planet.

About the Author

KENAN THOMPSON is an award-winning actor, comedian, and producer best known for his work on *Saturday Night Live*, where he is the longest-tenured cast member in the show's history.

Having joined the cast in 2003, Thompson has made countless contributions to *SNL* with his slew of hilarious impressions, including Rev. Al Sharpton, Charles Barkley, Steve Harvey, and David Ortiz, and memorable characters such as "Weekend Update" correspondent Jean K. Jean, "Black *Jeopardy!*" host Darnell Hayes, and Diondre Cole, the disruptive singing talk show host in the hit recurring sketch "What Up with That?"

Thompson has been nominated for six Emmy Awards for his work in television. In 2018 he won the Emmy for Outstanding Original Music and Lyrics for the *SNL* song "Come Back, Barack." In 2022 Thompson hosted the seventy-fourth Primetime Emmy Awards and was honored with a star on the Hollywood Walk of Fame.

Thompson made his television debut as an original cast member of Nickelodeon's all-kid sketch comedy series *All That*. He and Kel Mitchell debuted on the wildly popular spin-off *Kenan & Kel* in 1996 and starred in the fan-favorite 1997 *Good Burger* movie. Thompson served as an executive producer on Nickelodeon's 2019 *All That* reboot, and in 2023 he starred in *Good Burger 2*, the Paramount+ sequel to the original '90s film.

For two seasons, Thompson executive produced and starred as the title character in the NBC comedy series *Kenan*. Other television credits include *Bupkis*, *That Damn Michael Che*, *The Kids in the Hall*, *Bring the Funny*, and *Felicity*.

Recent film work includes *Bros*, *Clifford the Big Red Dog*, *Home Sweet Home Alone*, and *Hubie Halloween*. Additional film credits include *Going in Style*, *They Came Together*, starring opposite Samuel L. Jackson in *Snakes on a Plane*, *The Magic of Belle Isle* with Morgan Freeman, *Wieners*, *Barbershop 2: Back in Business*, *Fat Albert*, *My Boss's Daughter*, *D3: The Mighty Ducks*, *D2: The Mighty Ducks*, and *Heavyweights*. Thompson has lent his voice to animated films including *The Grinch*, *Trolls World Tour*, *Wonder Park*, *Space Chimps*, and *Rock Dog*.

In 2021 Thompson cofounded Artists for Artists, a full-service production and talent management company.

DUE DATE	MCN	11/23	30.00

DG

DISCARD